THE TIMES OF INDIA

DAAWAT
BASMATI RICE

PRESENTS

Finest Rice Recipes

SABINA SEHGAL SAIKIA

FIFTY DELECTABLE DISHES FROM BEST CHEFS

Finest Rice Recipes

First published in 2008

by

Bennett, Coleman & Co., Ltd.
7, Bahadur Shah Zafar Marg
New Delhi-110002

Editing, Design & Production: Times Group Books
Printed and Bound by : Lustra Print Process Pvt. Ltd.

ISBN 978-81-89960-16-0

Price: Rs.650

CONTENTS

EDITOR'S NOTE

It's a feast for the senses, yet it is a bridge between gluttony and lust. In certain cultures and particularly in these parts, rice — for good reason — is associated with fertility. It is synonymous with procreation, harvesting, longevity, divinity... each seamlessly flowing into the other. And like many an amorous — and divine — tale from India, Basmati is a matchless gift from the Indian subcontinent to the culinary world, the sensual world of feasting with the eyes, the nose, the palate, the texture and the sounds.

The question often asked is, where does taste end and aroma begin? Undoubtedly, the two are inseparable. For centuries, human ingenuity has stretched itself seeking the most delicate of fragrances. The Tantra has an entire section devoted to smells that ignite love. The seductive aroma of Basmati is embedded in its moniker itself — *bas* being aroma and *mati* translating into sense; a kind of ingrained aroma. In Hindi, Basmati simply connotes fragrance and refers to the sweet, natural aroma of this unique variety of rice.

Basmati is interwoven with the cultural ethos of the country like no other agricultural product... and the farming communities in India, in particular, have somewhat of a preordained claim over it. Quite like in the West, it is thrown on newly married couples as a symbol of fertility, luck and wealth. The interpretations are many and varied — some graphically sexual — but its potency and efficacy is clearly reflected in the burgeoning populations of India and China, where rice is the staple food.

Basmati, often referred to as the King of Rice, finds mention in Waris Shah's eighteenth-century epic poem *Heer Ranjha*:

Mushki chawalaan dey bharrey aan kothey,
Soyan pati tey jhoneray chari dey neen,
Basmati, Musafaree, Begumee soon Harchand de zardiay dhari de neen,
Suthee, karchaka sewala ghard, kanthal, anu kekala, sari dey neen,
Bareek safed Kashmir, Kabul khurush jeray hoor te pari dey neen....

The verse, roughly translated, reads:

Fragrant rice stores are filled, in which gold leafed and ordinary rice are being threshed,
Basmati, Musafaree, Begumee, Harchand and yellowish rice are getting stored,
Suthee, Karchaka, Sewala Ghard, Kanthal and Kekala rice are being moved,
Fine white Kashmir, Kabul rice dishes which are eaten by fairies and beautiful women....

This musk-scented rice has also been mentioned by Jean Baptiste Tavernier, a European traveller who described the rice fields seen by him on a journey from Surat (Gujarat, India) in 1654. He wrote, "All the rice grown in this country possesses a particular quality causing it to be much esteemed. Its grains are half as small as that of common rice, and when it is cooked, snow is not whiter than it is. Besides, it smells like musk and all the nobles of India eat no other. When you wish to make an acceptable present to anyone in Persia, you take him a sack of this rice." Yet another modern authority on rice, Dr Y L Nene points out that other than the mention by Waris Shah, other poets like Mushkin and Sukhdas have traced references to the "scented grain" back to Abul Fazl Allami's *Ain-e-Akbari*.

Ayurveda is replete with the healing, therapeutic powers of Basmati. The virtues and advice go thus: Basmati is the king of all rice varieties; it is *sattvik* or pure; it is nourishing for the body and easy to digest. Ayurveda recommends avoiding rice that is parboiled, instant or pre-cooked because it has less *prana* in it. Rice is generally good for balancing *Vata* and *Pitta*. Desserts made with rice and milk are particularly cooling and balancing for *Pitta*.

Indian Basmati, which predominantly grows on the foothills of the Himalayas, is also referred to as "White Gold". It is believed that the melting snows of the Himalayas, the rich soil and the right climate in the northern parts of the country are ideally suited to produce this distinctive quality of rice. While once associated with kings and royalty, it is today accessible to connoisseurs around the country. There is perhaps no celebration or special meal which does not feature Basmati in some form or the other — it is integral to an extraordinary meal.

Indeed, throughout history, it has been on royal menus of various cultures as the main dish. From the *pilav* of Turkey, *polou* of Persia, *pilaf*s of the Steppes, the *isoto*s and *paella*s of the Mediterranean, to the *pulao*s and *biryani*s of India, it has been served to great sultans, maharajahs, shahs and emperors. Spices, nuts, dried fruits, vegetables and herbs are natural embellishments for Basmati rice.

This compendium of recipes is a tribute to this unique and special rice variety that has pride of place in India and is recognized the world over. We, at the *Times of India*, would specially like to thank the distinguished chefs — indeed the stars of gastronomy in the country — who have generously shared their collective wisdom with us. And, of course, this book would not have been possible without the generous support of the Brothers Arora — Vijay Kumar and Ashwini — whose wonderful brand of Basmati, Daawat, bears testimony to the great culinary heritage we celebrate in this book.

I also take this opportunity to thank the team that assisted me in the actualization of this book. Aditya Jain, part-trainee part-adopted son, for following every last detail through. Subhasish Munshi, for implementing the aesthetic design of the book so competently, with the help of Balkishan Verma. Also the others in the team: Madhulita Mohanty, Soma B Chowdhury, Rupa Das, Aneesha Ganju and Manjula Natarajan. And especially, Sumanta Pal, who turned Basmati into Khasmati! Thank you all!

Sabina Sehgal Saikia
New Delhi

RICE LEGEND AND LORE: ABUNDANCE ABOUNDS

Like most legends, the story of rice is shrouded in a lot of myth and mystery, adding to its mystique. It is still not known exactly when and how people started growing rice; but archaeologists have uncovered evidence that rice was present in Indian civilizations as early as the seventh century BC, according to Tuk-Tuk Kumar, author of *The History of Rice in India*. She argues that rice husks used to temper clay pottery at the Koldihawa and Mahagara sites indicate that domesticated rice was grown at the time.

Other researchers document a slender, wild strain called *Indica* growing on the Himalayan slopes about 4,000 years ago. Extraordinary in yield, nutrition and resistance to disease, rice migrated around the globe with little promotion. Today, India's prized aromatic rice, Basmati, is found as far from its birthplace as Kenya and California. Though rightfully, quite like the French Champagne, India has contested and won the patent on the generic name of Basmati, which cannot be appropriated by other countries — which is why the Americans have been forced to refer to their Basmati variety of rice as Texmati!

And indeed, there are several references to rice being an integral part of India's ancient culture. Hindu scriptures have many references to rice. Kumar notes that the *Yajur Veda* describes the preparation of rice cakes as a ritual offering. In the *Atharva Veda*, rice, along with barley, is ascribed as being "a healing balm". The Smritis tell us of Goddess Devi Lalithambika, known to be especially fond of *payasa annam*, sweet rice. Indeed, husked rice is always present in even the simplest Hindu *puja* as one of the integral offerings. So revered is rice that, if mixed with turmeric powder, it often substitutes more opulent decorations for *murthis*.

Rice is also a potent symbol of auspiciousness and fertility in India. In the South, rice is referred to as Anna Lakshmi. Anna mean "food" and Lakshmi is the Goddess of Prosperity. From ancient times, Dhanya Lakshmi has been depicted holding a few sheaves of rice in her hand. The most special offering to Lord Ganesha is the *modakam*, a ball of sweet coconut/jaggery, covered with a thick rice paste. The first food fed to a child is rice. In Rajasthan, when a woman first enters her husband's house, a measure of rice is kept on the threshold. This is what she scatters through her new home, inviting prosperity and happiness. In South India, raw rice, mixed with *kumkum* to redden it, is known as *mangala akshadai* and showered over newly weds.

People in Gujarat celebrate Sharad Purnima by soaking flattened rice in sweet milk and drinking it at night. Drinking this *dood-powa* on this special night is said to protect health. In northern India, people celebrate the festival of Diwali with sugar candy, *batasha, maroondas* and *khil*, puffed rice. *The Rajah's Rice: A Mathematical Folktale from India*, by Barry David, contains an enchanting little tale of the young Chandra. By offering her the most expensive jewels in his kingdom as a reward for curing his sick elephants, the raja is captivated when young Chandra asks for one grain of rice, to be doubled for each square that is upon a chessboard. Her choice saves her village and cures the raja of his greed, all the while teaching students the concept of geometric progression.

Among Parsis, the Achu Michu ritual is performed to purify the mind and body of the bridal couple. Female members of the family carry two silver platters, each containing the following: eggs (symbolizing the life giving force), coconut (symbolizing inner and outer worlds), betel leaves and areca nuts (symbolizing suppleness and strength), unshelled almonds (symbolizing virtue and honesty), dried dates (symbolizing resilience), sugar crystals or sugar biscuits (symbolizing sweetness), dry rice (symbolizing abundance), rose petals (symbolizing happiness) and a glass of water (symbolizing purity, sanctity and perfection).

Etymologically too, the story of rice is full of abundant give-and-take.The Latin name for rice, *oryza*, is believed to have been borrowed from the Arabic traders who took it, ultimately, from the Sanskrit term *vrihi*. It is said that during the first *yuga* of this *manvantara*, people ate plain rice because it was so rich in nutrients and so sweet in taste. Just as virtue dominated the world, pure rice was the life-giver and people ate it unmixed with more earthy foods and apparently with perfect satisfaction. But with the second or *treta yuga*, people began to mix their rice with curds and certain vegetables, no longer satisfied with its simple pure taste. In the *dvapara* and *kali yuga* that followed, rice progressively was "mixed, covered, surrounded, adulterated and overwhelmed" by sauces, tangy vegetables, hot peppers or even meats. Rice by itself had gradually lost some of its nourishment and flavour, while the human appetite had become more aroused and voracious. In their custom of eating rice unseasoned in a dish separate from other seasoned foods, the Japanese are believed to have preserved something of an age-old awareness of the ideal.

Rice is the only food grain which does not sprout and hence when wet, does not decay as other food grains do. Rice cooked in ghee or clarified butter is said to have been the favourite food of the Prophet Muhammad. Rice also features in many legends about the Buddha's life. In Sanskrit, one of the words for rice is *dhaanya*, which roughly translates into "the sustainer of the human race". Shuddhodhana, the father of Gautama Buddha, was known as "pure rice" or, more literally, "pure gift". In a famous tale, the Buddha was offered a bowl of milk and rice by a young woman named Sujata, which gave him renewed strength during his austerities in pursuit of Enlightenment. It is for this reason that sweetened rice forms part of the offerings to the Buddha in Buddhist ceremonies.

Major harvest festivals include rice as an intrinsic ingredient: Pongal in Tamil Nadu, Onam in Kerala, Huthri in Coorg (Kodagu). Rice, tinted with the auspicious yellow colour of turmeric, is showered onto newly married couples and is part of numerous rites and celebrations. It is offered to deities and used as an oblation in the sacred fire of Hindu rituals. Rice is primarily a symbol of fertility and prosperity. Hindus particularly associate rice with Lakshmi, the Goddess of Prosperity. Paddy stalks or unhusked paddy is worshipped as embodying the goddess. The uses of rice in traditional medicine are closely interwoven with its use as a food.

Nepal's Jumli *marshi dhan* is a cold tolerant variety that is the world's highest growing rice cultivated at altitudes of nearly 3,000 metres. Every year, from October to December, the people around Ajingara Lake in Kapilavastu collect seeds called *tinna/tinni* rice that are eaten during the Chhat festival and on fasts like Ekadashi.

CHIEF CHARACTERISTICS OF BASMATI RICE

Origin: North India — the Basmati "Rice Bowl" — can stake its claim for gifting this precious offering to the culinary world. Basmati, which is grown in abundance in both India and Pakistan, is of the "premium" variety when sourced in India.

Colour: Traditionally, Basmati is considered to be at its best when it is translucent and creamy white, appropriately getting its *bon mot* of being "White Gold". Brown Basmati Rice is also available, and provides a healthy option, but it is white Basmati that is the most sought after.

Grain: What sets Basmati apart is the length of the grain. The grain is long (usually 6.61 to 7.50mm) or extra long (more than 7.50mm in length and 2mm in breadth).

Shape: Shape or length-to-width ratio is another criterion by which Basmati rice is identified. This needs to be over 3.0 in order to qualify as Basmati.

Texture: The beauty and distinctiveness of the Basmati grain is that it is dry, firm and separate. When cooked, the texture retains its firmness, even though it assumes tenderness without splitting, and, unlike other rice qualities, it is non-sticky, thanks to the amylose content in the rice. If the amylose value is anywhere between 20–22 per cent, cooked rice does not stick. The glutinous, sticky variety — often eaten with chopsticks — has 0–19 per cent amylose.

Elongation: One of the chief characteristics of Basmati rice is that it elongates almost twice upon cooking, but does not fatten significantly. The grains elongate on cooking (70–120 per cent over the pre-cooked grain), substantially more than other varieties.

Flavour: As aromatic as it is aesthetic in its appearance, it is the distinctive fragrance of Basmati that sets it apart. It is believed that the aroma in Basmati emanates from a cocktail of 100 compounds — hydrocarbons, alcohols, aldehydes and esters. A particular molecule of note is 2-acetyl-1-pyrroline.

Uses: Traditionally an ideal accompaniment to Indian curries and lentils, the flavour and texture of Basmati complements Indian food because it is a drier rice and the grains remain separate. It is also a wonderful rice for *biryanis* and *pilafs*, in which saffron heightens the Basmati experience with extra colour and flavour. It is a perfect rice for Indian and Middle Eastern cuisines.

COOKING BASMATI: TECHNICALLY SPEAKING

Rice when cooked — and each variety of rice requires its own special handling — absorbs water and swells during the process of cooking. This is due to the different proportion of starch and moisture that the rice contains, which produces varying degrees of softness/firmness and stickiness/separateness.

The cooking method greatly influences the quality of the cooked rice. Personally, I find that the rice cooker produces the best results — the grains are uniformly cooked and textured.

Broadly, there are four methods of cooking rice:

- The Absorption Method
- The Gentle Boil
- The Microwave Rice Cooker
- The Electric Rice Cooker

Cooking Basmati rice is no rocket science. It is a simple case of water assisting the rice to cook. In the Absorption Method, for instance, all you need to do is bring one cup of rice and one-and-a-half cups of water to the boil whilst stirring occasionally. The heat is then lowered to a medium/low level; the rice is covered with a lid and allowed to simmer for 15–20 minutes in the case of white rice, or 25–30 minutes for brown rice. The rice is then removed from the heat, and allow to stand covered for 5–10 minutes. It is recommended that you don't peek while the rice is covered with the lid.

Tip 1: For those who prefer firmer rice, it is suggested that the water added could be a little less and, for softer rice, slightly more could be added. Also, while cooking large quantities of rice, the amount of water-to-rice ratio should be reduced, largely because of the increased moisture which is produced while the rice is cooking.

Tip 2: A few drops of oil, butter or *desi* ghee and a teaspoon of fresh lime juice added during cooking helps the rice grains to remain separate and light during cooking. Stir-frying the rice in a little oil or *desi* ghee before adding water will also make the grains fluffy and separate.

The Gentle Boil method — also known as the "rapid boil" method — involves bringing one cup of rice and 6–8 cups of water to the boil, whilst stirring occasionally. The heat is lowered and the rice is brought to a gentle boil (as opposed to a vigorous rapid boil), and is cooked uncovered for 12–15 minutes in the case of white rice, or 25–30 minutes for brown rice. The rice is then removed from the heat and drained well.

Note: If the water is allowed to boil too vigorously, the grains will tend to split and the texture of the cooked rice will not be at its best. It is for this reason that a gentle boil is recommended over a vigorous boil.

While using a Microwave Rice Cooker, generally the same water-to-rice ratio as the absorption method is used. However, as different microwave ovens vary significantly, it is best to refer to the microwave oven manual for assistance.

The Electric Rice Cooker is an appliance that is extremely popular with Indians, primarily because it can produce a large quantity of rice that does not become mushy. Following the manufacturer's directions, place the rice and water in the cooker. Do not add salt. Cover and turn on the cooker. When the rice is done, the cooker will switch off automatically. It will turn on again at intervals to keep the rice hot. Do be careful that more than an hour of continuous heating can make the rice dry — it's best to serve it by then.

To rinse or not to rinse rice, that is the question

During the milling process, rice grains are gently rubbed against each other, leaving a fine powdery coating of starch on each grain. Also, rinsing all rice two to three times prior to cooking is recommended; this helps in removing any loose starch. For optimal cooking results, soaking — as opposed to rinsing — Basmati rice for 30 minutes prior to cooking is also recommended.

General cooking hints and tips

- Measure the water and rice accurately.
- Time the cooking accurately.
- Rinse the rice two to three times prior to cooking to remove any excess starch. There is no need to rinse rice after cooking.
- You can test if the rice is cooked *al dente* by pinching a grain. If there is no hard core or chalky centre, the rice is cooked.
- Do not rinse rice in a rice cooker especially if the rice cooker has a non-stick surface. The grains may scratch the cooker's surface.
- Always let cooked rice stand for 5–10 minutes off the heat, with the lid on, to complete the cooking process and redistribute the moisture evenly.
- Fluff cooked rice gently with a fork or flat plastic spoon provided with the rice cooker, for perfect fluffy rice. Slice through rice rather than stir it, to avoid the grains being mashed.
- Remember, the moisture content of rice can vary with age and storage conditions, so adjustments may have to be made to the amount of water added for cooking.

NUTRITIONAL NUGGETS: RICE IS RIGHT!

asmati ranks at the top for being the richest of all rice in amino acids and other essential nutrients, including iron, niacin, phosphorus, potassium, riboflavin and thiamine.

Rice is a wholesome and nutritious cereal grain and has qualities which make it ideally suited for special dietary needs.

- One cup of rice provides two servings of grain products.
- It is fat free. When cooked without salt, it is sodium free.
- It is high in dietary fibre and sodium free.
- It is a source of Vitamin E, folacin, zinc and potassium.
- It is a good source of pantothenic acid.
- It is an excellent source of thiamine, niacin, Vitamin B6, phosphorus, magnesium and iron.
- It is gluten free and non-allergenic.
- It is easy to digest.

With high nutrients, rice is a good source of insoluble fibre, which is also found in whole wheat, bran and nuts. Insoluble fibre reduces the risk of bowel disorders and fights constipation. Among other nutrients, rice is rich in carbohydrates, the main source of energy, low in fat, and contains some protein and plenty of Vitamin B.

Rice is an extremely healthy food for a number of reasons. Rice is a complex carbohydrate, which means that it contains starch and fibre. Complex carbohydrates are digested slowly, allowing the body to utilise the energy released over a longer period, which is nutritionally efficient.

Rice has low sodium content and contains useful quantities of potassium, the B vitamins, thiamine and niacin. An average portion of rice (50g) provides about 11 per cent of the average daily requirement of protein. One portion of Basmati rice — one cup — accounts for roughly 170–205 kcal; 4.2g of protein; 44.5g of carbohydrate; total fat of 0.44g and fibre of 0.63g. It is also a good source of protein iron (1.9mg), selenium (11.8mcg), thiamine (0.26mg), and niacin (2.3mg). Those looking to reduce their fat and cholesterol intakes can turn to rice because it contains only a trace of fat and no cholesterol at all. Rice is also gluten free, and is suitable for coeliacs; it is easily digested, and a wonderful food both for the very young and elderly.

Incidentally, rice, brown rice in particular, complements both vegetarian and vegan dishes.

GOSHT BIRYANI

CHEF RAJESH WADHWA, TAJ PALACE HOTEL, DELHI

To serve: 5
Preparation time: 45 minutes
Cooking time: 1 hour 30 minutes

Ingredients

Biryani rice: 4cups
Lamb (curry cut): 1kg
Olive oil: ¼cup
Cloves: 2-3
Green cardamom: 3-4
Bay leaves: 3
Cinnamon: 3 sticks
Browned onion: ½cup
Ginger-garlic paste: 5tbsp
Yoghurt: 2/3cup
Salt to taste
Yellow chilli powder: 2½tsp
Saffron: a pinch
Cream: ¼cup
Mint leaves: ½ a bunch
Mace-cardamom powder: ½tsp
Chopped coriander leaves: 1tsp
Kewra water: 2-3 drops

Method

Wash and soak rice for half an hour. Then boil in water till three-fourth done. Strain the water and reserve the rice.

Heat oil in a *handi* and crackle whole garam masala. Then add the lamb pieces with fried onions, ginger-garlic paste and salt. Sauté.

Add a little water and cook till done.

Sprinkle salt, chilli powder, cumin powder, mace-cardamom powder, saffron, green chillies and mint leaves. Sauté.

Then add the beaten yoghurt and the cooked lamb.

Finish with cream and adjust the seasoning.

Take a separate *patila* and arrange some rice on the base. Put the cooked lamb on the rice and top with another layer of rice.

Now garnish with chopped coriander, browned onions and mint leaves.

Seal the lid with dough and put on *dum* for 10 minutes.

Remove the lid and serve with Raita.

GOSHT AWADH BIRYANI

CHEF GULAM M QURESHI, ITC MAURYA, DELHI

To serve: 4

Preparation time: 30 minutes

Cooking time: 1 hour 15 minutes

Ingredients

Mutton: 800gm
Browned onion: 2tbsp
Cloves: 5
Bay leaves: 2
Cream: ¼cup
Yellow chilli powder: 2tsp
Ginger-garlic paste: 2tbsp
Kewra water: 1tsp
Slit green chilli: 1tbsp
Ginger julienne: 1tbsp
Lemon juice: 1tbsp
Dough for sealing
Salt to taste
Basmati rice: 2cups
Desi ghee: 2tbsp
Cinnamon: 5sticks
Green cardamom: 2tsp
Beaten yoghurt: ½cup
Mace and cardamom powder: 1tsp
Rose water: 1tsp
Sweet ittar: 1drop
Mint leaves: 1tbsp
Royal cumin seeds: 1tsp
Water: 1½litre
Saffron: a pinch

Method

Heat ghee in a copper vessel or *lagan* and add the whole spices. When they crackle, add the mutton pieces and sauté.

Sprinkle salt over the mutton pieces.

Add ginger-garlic paste and some brown onions. Sauté again for a while.

Add beaten yoghurt and sauté till the oil separates. Next, add yellow chilli powder and mace-cardamom powder.

Pour in water and cook. Keep aside.

Wash and soak rice for 10 minutes.

Boil water in a pan and add the whole spices, salt and lemon juice.

Add the rice and cook till about 70 per cent done.

In a large vessel, make alternate layers using the cooked mutton and the boiled rice.

Add a mixture of ghee and cream on top.

Garnish with mint leaves, ginger juliennes, the remaining brown onion and saffron dissolved in water.

Line the lid with dough and seal the vessel.

Put the vessel on an iron *tawa* and cook on *dum* for 15 minutes.

KACCHE GOSHT KI BIRYANI

Chef Chalapathi Rao, ITC Kakatiya, Hyderabad

To serve: 4

Preparation time: 1 hour 30 minutes

Cooking time: 1 hour 15 minutes

Ingredients

Mutton: 1kg
Garlic paste: ½cup
Red chilli powder: as required
Cardamom: ½cup (half whole, half powdered)
Beaten yoghurt: 1¼cup
Chopped mint leaves: 2bunches
Browned onion: 10cups
Basmati rice: 3cups
Dough for sealing
Ginger paste: 1cup
Salt to taste
Cinnamon: ½cup (half whole, half powdered)
Cloves: ¼cup (half whole, half powdered)
Chopped coriander leaves: 2bunches
Slit green chilli: 1½tbsp
Clarified fat or butter: 1kg

Method

Wash the mutton thoroughly and drain away the excess water.

Wash the rice about three times and soak it for a duration of 10–15 minutes.

Place the mutton in a *lagan*. Thoroughly mix in ginger paste, garlic paste, salt, red chilli powder, whole cinnamon, cardamom and cloves.

Allow the flavours to seep into the mutton for a while.

After a while, add the yoghurt, green chillies, coriander and mint leaves to the mutton.

Also mix in the onions and about half of the amount of clarified fat.

Adjust the seasoning and finish it by adding cinnamon powder, cardamom powder, clove powder and the remaining clarified fat.

In a *handi*, allow water to boil. When it begins to boil, add salt, whole cinnamon, cardamom and cloves.

Pick, wash and soak the rice. Now add the rice to this flavoured water and cook till it is 70 per cent done.

Spread the rice on the meat in the *lagan*.

Now seal the *lagan* and place it on a *tawa* on a high flame. When the steam starts escaping, reduce the flame and cook on *dum* for approximately 40 minutes.

Dredge the remaining quantity of the clarified fat on the rice. Garnish the rice with chopped coriander leaves, slit green chillies and browned onion.

Serve with Dahi ki Chutney and Mirch ka Salan.

YAKHNI PULAO

CHEF AMIT CHOWDHURY, THE TAJ MAHAL HOTEL, DELHI

To serve: 5
Preparation time: 20 minutes
Cooking time: 45 minutes

Ingredients

Basmati rice: 2½cups
Beaten yoghurt: ½cup
Sliced onion: 2onions
Chilli powder: ½tsp
Cinnamon: 2 sticks
Black peppercorn: 10-12
Cumin seeds: ½tsp
Whole coriander seeds: 1/3tsp
Cloves: 6
Dough for sealing
Mutton: 500gm
Ginger-garlic paste: ¼cup
Ghee: ½cup
Green cardamom: 7-8
Black cardamom: 2-3
Fennel seeds: ½tsp
Mace: 3-4
Bay leaves: 3-4
Salt to taste

Method

Take the mutton, half the ginger-garlic paste, 1½ litres of water and salt and boil in a *patila* or pressure cooker.

Tie the cinnamon, black and green cardamoms, cloves, mace, peppercorns, coriander, fennel seeds, cumin seeds, bay leaves and red chilli powder in a piece of muslin cloth.

Put this bundle in the pan along with the mutton.

Simmer till the mutton is done. Strain the liquid and keep the mutton stock or *yakhni* and mutton pieces separately.

Meanwhile, wash the rice and soak in water for 30 minutes.

Heat ghee in a pan and fry the sliced onions until golden brown.

Add the other half of the ginger-garlic paste, bay leaves, mace and small cardamoms. Sauté for a while.

Add beaten yoghurt and sauté further. Then add *yakhni* from the boiled pieces and boil for some time.

Now add the soaked rice and bring to a boil. Then simmer for a while. When it is half cooked, add the cooked mutton pieces and salt.

Seal the lid of the pan with dough. Put the vessel on *dum* in a preheated oven for 10–12 minutes.

Leave aside for a few minutes. Open the seal and serve hot.

CHOOZA BIRYANI

CHEF GULAM M QURESHI, ITC MAURYA, DELHI

To serve: 4

Preparation time: 30 minutes

Cooking time: 45 minutes-1 hour

Ingredients

Chooza (spring chicken of 150-200gm): 4
Browned onion: 3tbsp
Cloves: 5
Bay leaves: 5
Cream: ¼cup
Yellow chilli powder: 1tsp
Ginger-garlic paste: 1tbsp
Kewra water: 1tsp
Slit green chilli: 1½tsp
Ginger julienne: 3tbsp
Lemon juice: 1tbsp
Dough for sealing
Salt to taste
Basmati rice: 2cups
Desi ghee: ½cup
Cinnamon: 5sticks
Green cardamom: 2tsp
Beaten yoghurt: ½cup
Mace-cardamom powder: 1tsp
Rose water: 1tsp
Sweet ittar: 2drops
Mint leaves: 1tbsp
Royal cumin seeds: 1tsp
Water: ½litre
Saffron: a pinch

Method

Heat ghee in a *lagan* and add the whole spices. When they crackle, add ginger-garlic paste and browned onions and sauté again for a while.

After a few minutes, add beaten yoghurt and sauté till the oil separates.

Add the *chooza* to this masala and fry for a while. Now put yellow chilli powder and mace-cardamom powder.

Pour in the water and cook the *chooza* by putting the vessel on *dum*.

Meanwhile, wash and soak the rice for 10 minutes. Boil water in a pan and add the whole spices, salt and lemon juice.

Add the rice and cook till about 70 per cent done.

Layer the cooked *chooza* with the boiled rice.

Garnish with mint leaves, ginger juliennes, brown onions and saffron dissolved in water.

Line the lid with dough and seal the vessel. Cook on *dum* for 10 minutes.

Serve hot with yoghurt.

KEEMA BHARA MURG MUSALLAM PULAO

CHEF ANURAG BALI, THE CLARIDGES, DELHI

To serve: 6
Preparation time: 30 minutes
Cooking time: 50 minutes

Ingredients

Long grain Basmati rice: 2½cups
Minced chicken: 250gm
Mint leaves: 2 sprigs
Cloves: 5
Cinnamon: 2 small sticks
Whole chicken: 1kg
Eggs: 2
Milk: ½cup
Green cardamom: 5

For mince

Ghee: ½cup
Royal cumin seeds: ½tsp
Chopped green chilli: 1tbsp
Red chilli powder: 2tsp
Yoghurt: ¼cup
Chopped onion: ¾cup
Ginger-garlic paste: 4tsp
Turmeric powder: 1tsp
Coriander powder: 1tbsp
Salt to taste

For whole chicken

Ginger-garlic paste: 3tbsp
Hung yoghurt: 3tbsp
Browned onion paste: 1tbsp
Turmeric powder: 1tsp
Garam masala: ½tsp
Chopped green chilli: 1tbsp
Chicken stock: 2cups
Salt to taste
Lemon: 1
Browned cashew nut paste: 1tbsp
Kewra water: a few drops
Yellow chilli powder: 1tsp
Red chilli powder: 1tsp
Ghee: ½cup
Saffron: a few strands

Method

Pick, wash and soak the rice for half an hour.

Heat ghee in a *lagan*. Splutter royal cumin seeds and add chopped onions. Sauté till light golden. Add ginger-garlic paste, turmeric powder, red chilli powder, coriander powder and salt. Sauté for a while and add yoghurt. Cook.

Once the moisture evaporates, add chicken mince and cook till done. Keep aside. Separately hard boil an egg, peel it and keep aside.

Clean the whole chicken and put incisions on the breast and leg.

Smear salt, ginger-garlic paste and lemon juice on the chicken and keep aside for half an hour.

Mix the browned cashew and onion pastes. To it, add hung yoghurt, salt, kewra water, turmeric powder, yellow chilli powder, red chilli powder, chopped green chillies and garam masala.

Stuff the chicken using half the mince and the boiled egg. Tie the chicken securely with a thread. Now heat ghee in a *lagan* and cook the stuffed chicken on low heat. Add chicken stock, cover and cook till done.

Boil water, add salt and rice and parboil. Drain the water and keep the rice aside.

In a separate *lagan*, layer the rice and the remaining mince. Pour a little ghee on top, cover and cook for 10 minutes on simmer.

Dish out the rice and place the whole chicken on the rice. Serve hot with raita.

MAHI RASEELI BIRYANI

Chef Gurpreet Gedhu, Delhi 'O' Delhi, India Habitat Centre, Delhi

To serve: 4
Preparation time: 30 minutes
Cooking time: 15 minutes

Ingredients

River sole tikka: eight 2inch cubes
Basmati rice: 2cups
Onion: 2 medium sized
Ghee: 1 ladle
Red chilli powder: 2tsp
Chopped coriander: 6tsp
Rice powder: 6tsp
Dough for sealing
Fenugreek seeds: 4tsp
Ginger-garlic paste: a 1inch ginger and 2 pods of garlic
Beaten yoghurt: 2cups
Turmeric powder: 1tsp
Coriander powder: 2tsp
Fish bones: 1 carcass of a medium-sized fish
Salt to taste

Method

Heat ghee in a *handi* and sauté fenugreek seeds till they turn golden brown.
Then add onions and cook till the onions turn brown.
Sauté ginger-garlic paste, salt, red chilli powder, turmeric powder and coriander powder for a minute and add beaten yoghurt.
After a couple of minutes, add fish bones and 2 litres of water. Simmer for half an hour and strain the stock.
Now dip the fish in a batter of salt, red chilli powder, turmeric powder, lemon juice, ginger-garlic paste and rice powder and fry in a separate pan.
Now add the fried fish to the stock along with chopped coriander leaves. Check the seasoning by adding cumin powder and garam masala.
Cook the rice separately till it is 80 per cent done.
In the biryani pot, put a layer of stock, rice, fried fish, chopped coriander and browned onion.
Put some more rice and thick stock. Garnish with chopped coriander leaves and browned onion.
Cook on *dum* for 7 minutes.

JHINGA BIRYANI

CHEF ANDREW WHIFFEN, THE OBEROI, DELHI

To serve: 10
Preparation time: 45 minutes
Cooking time: 1-1½ hours

Ingredients

Deheaded and deveined medium prawns (jhinga): 1½kg
Basmati rice: 3cups
Mace: ½tsp
Cloves: ½tsp
Ghee: 1cup
Garlic paste: 2tbsp
Mace: ½tsp
Coriander powder: 1tbsp
Salt to taste
Chopped tomato: 6-8 medium sized tomatoes
Saffron (soaked in hot milk): a pinch
Ginger julienne: 2tbsp
Chopped mint leaves: 2tbsp
Cardamom powder: 1tsp
Milk (to soak saffron): ½cup
Cardamom: ½tsp
Bay leaf: 1
Cinnamon: ½tsp
Ginger paste: 4tbsp
Green cardamom: 1tsp
Red chilli powder: 2tsp
Turmeric powder: 2tsp
Finely sliced onion: 12 medium-sized onions
Beaten yoghurt: 1cup
Cream: ½cup
Chopped coriander leaves: 4tbsp
Green chilli julienne: 2tsp
Mace powder: ½tsp
Dough for sealing

Method

Marinate the prawns with half the ginger-garlic paste, salt, red chilli powder and turmeric powder and leave for half an hour.

In a *kadai*, heat ghee. Splutter cardamom and mace and stir for 30 seconds on a slow fire.

Add sliced onions and fry till they turn brown.

Add ginger and garlic pastes and stir for a minute on a slow fire.

Sprinkle red chilli powder, turmeric powder and coriander powder. Stir for 30 seconds on a slow fire.

Mix in chopped tomatoes.

Add marinated prawns, mix and simmer for 5 minutes.

Add beaten yoghurt, mix and bring to a boil. Simmer for 10 minutes

In a separate container, boil water with salt and whole garam masala.

Add washed and soaked rice, bring to a boil and simmer until the rice is three-fourth cooked.

Strain the water.

In a heavy-bottomed *patila*, place the cooked prawns. Then sprinkle chopped coriander, chopped mint, ginger and green chilli juliennes and browned onions.

Pour 2 tablespoons each of melted butter and ghee.

Now sprinkle some saffron, cardamom powder and mace powder.

Place the first layer of rice and put saffron, browned onion, butter and cream on top of the rice. Place the second layer of rice.

Top it with more saffron and butter. Cover with a clean wet kitchen duster, seal the lid with dough and cook on *dum* over slow fire for 20–25 minutes. Serve with Raita or Kachumber salad.

LOTUS BIRYANI

Chef Shivanand Kain, Jaypee Siddharth, Delhi

To serve: 6

Preparation time: 30 minutes

Cooking time: 1 hour

Ingredients

Basmati rice: 1kg
Phool makhana: 50gm
Ghee: 10tbsp
Red chilli powder: 1tbsp
Brown onion paste: 2cups
Seasoning to taste
Cinnamon: 1 large stick
Black cardamom: 3
Black peppercorn: ½tsp
Mint leaves: 2tbsp
Nutmeg powder: 1tsp
Green chilli: 4
Lotus stem: 1kg
Ginger julienne: 2inch piece
Ginger-garlic paste: 1½tbsp
Coriander powder: 1tbsp
Yoghurt: 1cup
Green cardamom: 3
Bay leaves: 2
Cloves: 5
Lotus flower: 1
Saffron: a pinch
Mace powder: 1tsp
Dough for sealing

Method

Heat ghee in a large pan. Add ginger-garlic paste, peeled and sliced lotus stems, red chilli powder and coriander powder. Sauté.

Now add brown onion paste and yoghurt. Check the seasoning.

Boil the rice separately with green cardamom, black cardamom, cinnamon, bay leaves, cloves and black pepper. When almost done, keep aside.

Arrange the biryani in a vessel with lotus leaves on the sides. Put alternate layers of *nadroo* (lotus stem) masala, fried makhana and cooked rice garnished with mint leaves, green chillies and ginger juliennes.

Seal the lid of the vessel with dough and let it cook on a slow fire for 4–5 minutes.

Before serving, top with saffron water, nutmeg and mace powder. Serve garnished with ginger juliennes and slit green chillies.

SANGRI AND MANGORI PULAO

CHEF RAKESH GHAI, SHERATON RAJPUTANA HOTEL, JAIPUR

To serve: 4
Preparation time: 15 minutes
Cooking time: 30 minutes

Ingredients

Rice: 2¼cups
Mangori: 1cup
Sangri: ½cup
Green chilli: 2tsp
Ginger: 2tsp
Mint leaves: 3½tbsp
Cream: 3½tbsp
Milk: 500ml
Butter: 2tbsp
Desi ghee: ½cup
Saffron: a pinch
Salt to taste
Dough for sealing

Method

Parboil rice.
Deep fry the mangoris till golden brown and boil sangri.
Prepare a mixture of cream, butter, milk, desi ghee and saffron.
Take a *lagan* and put into it rice, mangori and sangri.
Pour the cream mixture on top of the rice.
Keep it on *dum* for 5 minutes.
Serve hot.

PUNJABI PYAAZA PULAO

CHEF YOGESH ARORA, TIFFIN ROOM, RAFFLES HOTEL, SINGAPORE

To serve: 4-6

Preparation time: 45 minutes

Cooking time: 25-35 minutes

Ingredients

Basmati rice: 1cup
Sliced red onion: 2-3 large onions
Chopped garlic: 4-6 cloves
Chopped ginger: 1inch stick
Cumin seeds: ½tsp
Fresh milk: ½cup
Cinnamon: 1 stick
Green cardamom: 6
Black cardamom: 2
Bay leaves: 2
Cloves: 4
Ghee: ½cup
Water: 1cup
Sea salt to taste

Method

Wash, soak the rice and keep aside.

Heat ghee and splutter the whole spices.

Stir-fry for a while and add cumin seeds. Stir-fry again till the cumin seeds crackle.

Now add garlic and sauté till the garlic turns golden.

Fry the onions till they turn translucent.

Next, stir-fry the ginger for a few minutes and add the pre-soaked and washed rice.

Stir all the ingredients together to let the rice absorb all the flavours.

Add water and fresh milk to the rice. Stir and cook on a slow to medium heat for 8–10 minutes.

Once cooked, remove the pulao from the fire and serve hot.

SUBZ TEHRI

CHEF RAJESH WADHWA, TAJ PALACE HOTEL, DELHI

To serve: 5

Preparation time: 35-40 minutes

Cooking time: 25 minutes

Ingredients

Biryani rice: 4cups
Carrot: 1
Green peas: ½cup
Cauliflower florets: ½cup
Beans: ½cup
Yellow chilli powder: 1tbsp
Green chilli powder: ½tsp
Cream: 2½tbsp
Chopped mint: 1tsp
Chopped coriander leaves: 1½tsp
Olive oil: ¼cup
Cumin powder: 1tsp
Saffron: a pinch
Cumin seeds: 1tsp
Mace-cardamom powder: ½tsp
Salt to taste
Dough for sealing

Method

Wash vegetables and cut into dices. Blanch and keep aside.

Wash and soak rice for half an hour and boil in water till three-fourth done. Strain the water and reserve the rice.

Now heat oil in a pan and crackle cumin seeds.

Next, add diced and blanched vegetables.

Add salt, chilli powder, green chilli, cumin powder, mace-cardamom powder, saffron and mint and sauté.

Finish with cream and adjust the seasoning.

Take a pot, arrange some rice on the base, and put a layer of sautéed vegetables.

Top with a layer of rice.

Now garnish with chopped coriander leaves and mint leaves.

Sealed the lid with dough and put on *dum* for 10 minutes.

Remove the lid and serve with Raita.

GUCCHI BIRYANI

CHEF RAJESH WADHWA, TAJ PALACE HOTEL, DELHI

To serve: 5

Preparation time: 35-40 minutes

Cooking time: 25 minutes

Ingredients

Biryani rice: 4cups

Yellow chilli powder: 2tsp

Salt to taste

Chopped green chilli: 3 small chillies

Cream: 1½tbsp

Chopped mint leaves: 1tsp

Chopped coriander leaves: 1tsp

Olive oil: ¼cup

Cumin powder: 1tsp

Saffron: a pinch

Cumin seeds: 1tsp

Mace-cardamom powder: ½tsp

Gucchi (morels): ½cup

Browned onion: ½cup

Method

Wash and soak rice for half an hour. Then boil rice in water till three-fourth done. Strain the water and reserve the rice.

Soak gucchi in water. When soft, cut into slices.

Now heat oil in a pan, crackle cumin seeds and add sliced gucchi.

Season with salt, chilli powder, green chillies, cumin powder, mace-cardamom powder, saffron and mint. Sauté.

Finish with cream and adjust the seasoning.

Take a pot, arrange some rice on the base and then put a layer of sautéed gucchi on the rice. Top with rice again.

Now garnish with chopped coriander and mint leaves.

Seal the lid with dough and put on *dum* for 10 minutes.

Remove the lid and serve with Raita.

MOOPLAH ERRAICHI BIRYANI

Chef Manisha Bhasin, Sheraton, Delhi

To serve: 5

Preparation time: 1 hour

Cooking time: 1 hour

Ingredients

Prawns: 500gm
Ghee: ½cup
Cashew nut: 2tbsp
Chopped onion: 1/2cup
Coriander powder: 2tsp
Coriander leaves: 1tbsp
Green cardamom: 5
Chopped tomato: ½cup
Ginger-garlic paste: 2tbsp
Lemon: 2
Dough for sealing
Basmati rice: 2½cups
Turmeric powder: 2tsp
Sultana: 2tbsp
Red chilli powder: 2tsp
Mint leaves: 2tsp
Cinnamon: 5sticks
Cloves: 5
Yoghurt: 1cup
Split green chilli: 2tsp
Salt to taste

Method

Marinate the prawns with turmeric, salt and lemon juice for half an hour.

Wash the rice and sauté it in ghee for 5 minutes. Add salt, turmeric powder and lukewarm water.

Bring the rice to a boil, lower the heat and cover the *patila*.

Heat ghee in a separate pan and add sultanas and cashew nuts.

Fry till they turn golden brown and keep aside.

Add onion in the same oil and sauté till they turn golden brown. Sprinkle chilli powder, coriander powder and turmeric powder and pour in a cup of water. Fry for 2 minutes.

Add in the marinated prawns and sauté for 5 minutes.

Then add yoghurt, tomatoes and water. Allow to simmer for another 5 minutes.

Next, pour in the cooked rice with the sultanas and cashew nuts.

Put mint leaves and coriander leaves on top.

Cover the *patila* with a lid and seal with dough.

Put the *patila* on a hot plate or slow fire for 5 minutes.

Serve with Onion Pachdi.

KOZHI PULAO

CHEF SANDEEP KACHROO, THE TAJ WEST END, BANGALORE

To serve: 4

Preparation time: 25 minutes

Cooking time: 30 minutes

Ingredients

Chicken: 600gm
Refined oil: ½cup
Cinnamon: 2 sticks
Marathi moong: 2
Ginger paste: 1tsp
Yoghurt: ½cup
Slit green chilli: 6
Coriander powder: 1tsp
Chopped coriander leaves: 1tbsp
Salt: ½tsp
Water: 3cup
Basmati rice: 2cups
Green cardamom: 4
Cloves: 2
Bay leaves: 2
Garlic paste: 1tsp
Sliced onion: 4
Chopped tomato: 2
Garam masala powder: 1tsp
Chopped mint leaves: 1tbsp
Ghee: 4tbsp

Method

Wash and soak the rice.

Place a thick-bottomed vessel on medium flame and heat oil in it. When the oil becomes hot, add all the whole spices to crackle.

Sauté sliced onions till they turn translucent.

Add in ginger and garlic pastes and sauté till the paste is cooked.

Put in the green chillies and tomatoes and cook for 5 minutes. Now add coriander powder and cook for 15 seconds.

Add chicken and cook till the chicken is half done. To the chicken, add powdered garam masala, mint, coriander leaves, yoghurt and salt. Cook till the oil comes to the top. Add water.

Once the water starts boiling, add the soaked rice and cook till three-fourth of the water has evaporated. Now add ghee, seal the vessel with a tight lid and cook on a hot plate for 14 minutes.

Take the vessel off the flame and serve hot with Raita or Salan.

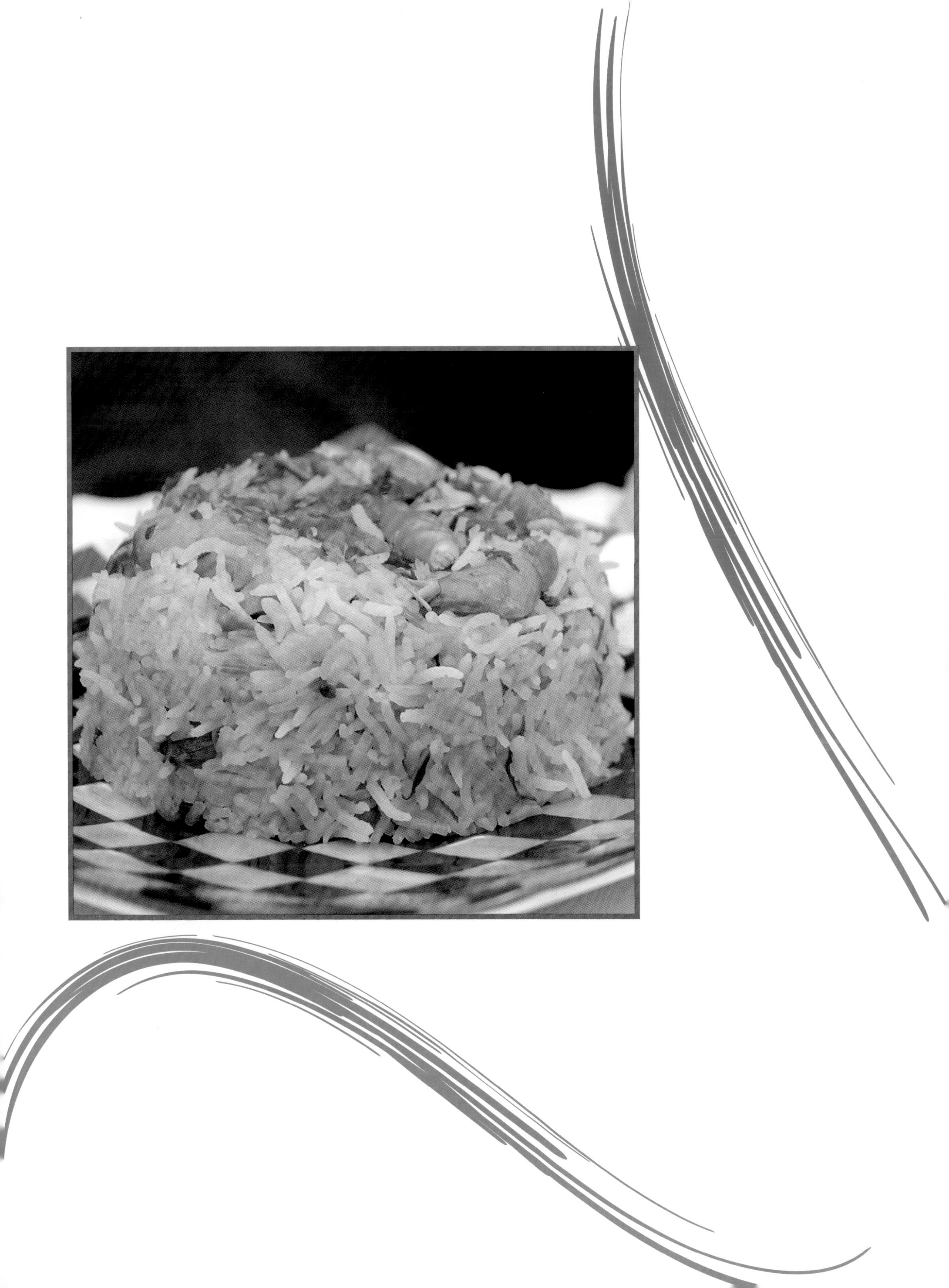

TOMATO RICE

CHEF HEMANT OBEROI, THE TAJ MAHAL PALACE & TOWER, MUMBAI

To serve: 4

Preparation time: 20 minutes

Cooking time: 20 minutes

Ingredients

Tomato: 4 medium-sized tomatoes
Basmati rice: 1¼cup
Chopped onion: 2
Finely chopped ginger: 1inch root
Chilli powder: 1tsp
Coriander powder: ½tsp
Cumin powder: ½tsp
Turmeric powder: ½tsp
Garam masala powder: 1/3tsp
Oil: ¼cup
Coriander leaves: 1tsp
Mustard seeds: ½tsp
Salt to taste

Method

Wash and soak the rice. Keep aside.

Heat oil in a pan and add the mustard seeds. When it starts spluttering, add onions and fry till they turn translucent.

Add ginger, tomatoes, salt and turmeric and keep stirring.

When all the ingredients are mixed together, add all the dry masalas.

Cook, stirring frequently.

When the tomatoes are cooked, add 500ml of water.

Add the soaked rice and combine well.

Cover with a lid and cook till the rice is done.

Garnish with fresh coriander leaves.

VEGETABLE BRINJI

CHEF NABOJIT GHOSH, TAJ COROMANDEL, CHENNAI

To serve: 4
Preparation time: 20 minutes
Cooking time: 25 minutes

Ingredients

Basmati rice: 2cups
Diced onion: 2 large onions
Assorted vegetables (carrots, beans, potatoes, green peas, double beans): 1½cup
Diced tomato: 2 small tomatoes
Slit green chilli: 1tsp
Mint leaves: ½ a bunch
Coriander leaves: ½ a bunch
Ginger-garlic paste: 1tsp
Ghee: ½cup
Whole garam masala: 1tsp
Bay leaves: 4
Star anise: 2-3
Peeled garlic: ½tsp
Cashew nut: ½tsp
Yoghurt: 1cup
Coconut milk: 1cup
Salt to taste
Crotons to garnish

Method

Soak rice for 20 minutes and keep aside.

Take ghee in a small *handi* and heat it. Add all the dry spices to the ghee. Let them crackle.

Now put diced onions and sauté well. After that, put in slit green chillies, chopped mint leaves and coriander leaves.

Sauté and put ginger-garlic paste followed by tomatoes.

Season with chilli powder, coriander powder, turmeric powder and salt.

Sauté well and add all the vegetables.

Pour in water so that its quantity is equal to that of the vegetables.

Let the vegetables cook to half. Then slowly put the soaked rice on top of the vegetables.

Pour some coconut milk on top and seal the *handi* with dough. Put it on a hot plate or over a low flame. Let it cook for 15–20 minutes.

Now remove the lid and garnish with big crotons and fried cashew nuts.

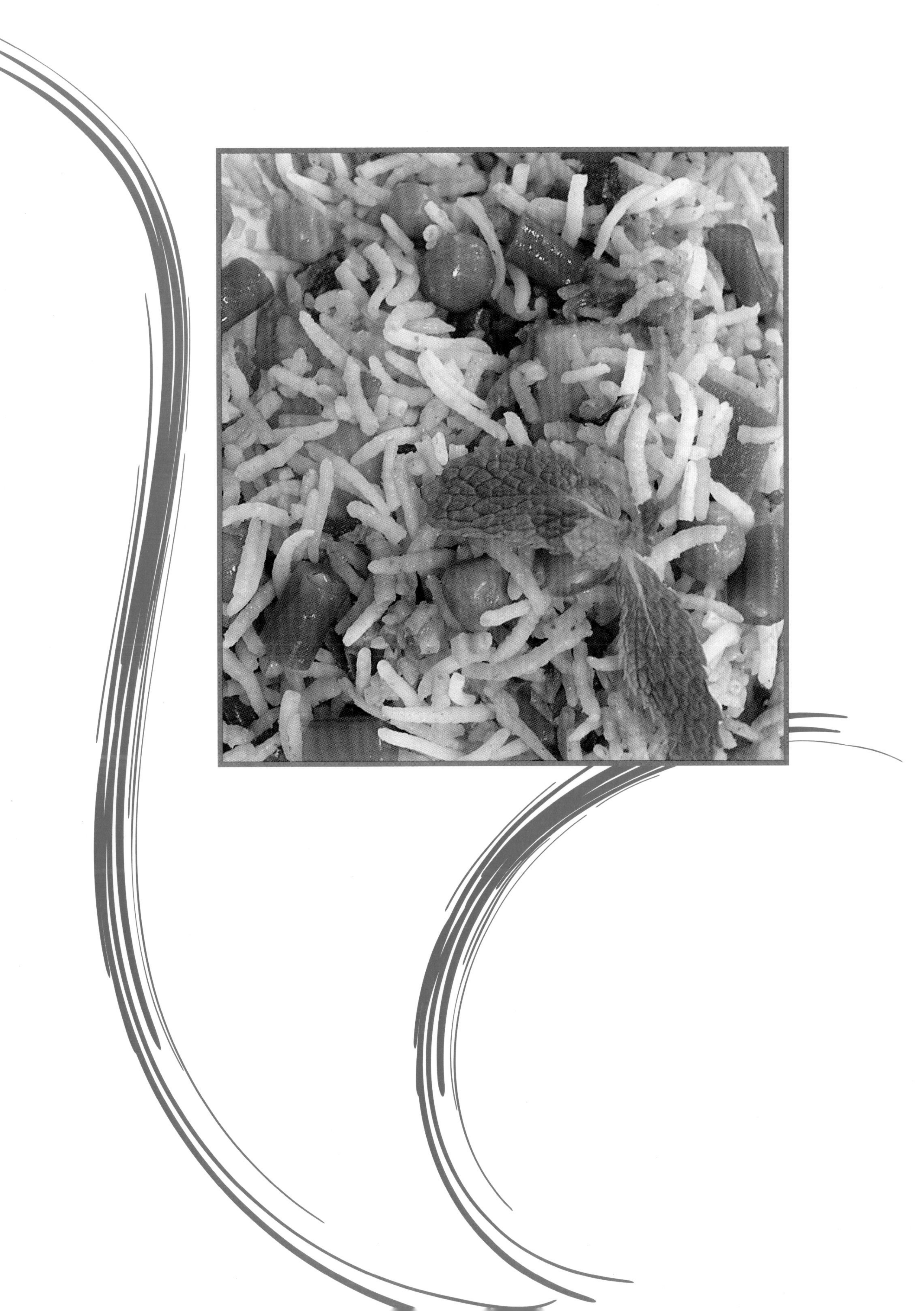

PULIYODARAI

Chef Praveen Anand, ITC Hotel Park Sheraton & Towers, Chennai

To serve: 2

Preparation time: 45 minutes

Cooking time: 15 minutes

Ingredients

Rice: 1½cup
Water: 2¼litres
Tamarind: 1cup
Gingelly oil (til ka tel): for tempering
Red chilli: 3tbsp
Mustard seeds: 2tsp
Fenugreek seeds: ½tsp
Turmeric powder: 1tsp
Peanut: 1½tbsp
Curry leaves: a few sprigs
Salt to taste

Method

Wash, strain and boil rice, allow it to cool.

Soak, mix well and make an extract of tamarind. Strain.

Make a tempering with gingelly oil, red chilli, mustard seeds, fenugreek seeds, turmeric powder, peanuts and curry leaves.

Pour in the tamarind extract and cook on medium heat till it reduces to half.

Check seasoning. Remove and add to the rice.

Mix well and serve hot.

QOOBOLI

CHEF CHALAPATHI RAO, ITC KAKATIYA, HYDERABAD

To serve: 4
Preparation time: 45 minutes
Cooking time: 45 minutes

Ingredients

Basmati rice: 3cups
Finely chopped onions: 2cups
Ginger paste: ¾cup
Garlic paste: ½cup
Yoghurt: 2¼cups
Salt to taste
Red chilli powder: 1tbsp
Turmeric powder: 1½tsp
Cinnamon: 1tbsp
Cardamon: 1tbsp
Cloves: 2tsp
Chana dal: 2½cups
Chopped coriander: 1bunch
Coarsely chopped mint: 1bunch
Slit green chilli: 2tsp
Clarified fat: 2½cups

Method

In a preheated *lagan*, put in clarified fat. Add processed onions and cook until they are brown.

Add processed ginger and garlic and cook until the flavours amalgamate with the base.

Put yoghurt and cook until the raw flavour of this ingredient has been masked. Season it with salt, red chilli powder, turmeric powder, processed cinnamon, cardamon and cloves to get a good flavour.

Add processed coriander.

Add Basmati rice to a *handi* with water that is boiling and is flavoured with whole cinnamon, cardamom, cloves and salt.

Cook the rice until it is 70 per cent done. Layer the rice in a *lagan*, alternating it with the gravy that was processed earlier.

Dredge the rice with the remaining quantity of clarified fat. Seal it with a lid enforced with lute and cook upon a hot plate or a *tawa,* utilizing a moderate flame until steam comes out. This would take 25–30 minutes.

Garnish with finely chopped coriander leaves, slit green chillies, fried raisins and blanched walnuts. Pyaaz ki Chutney is a good accompaniment.

JODHPURI PULAO

CHEF RAKESH GHAI, SHERATON RAJPUTANA HOTEL, JAIPUR

To serve: 4
Preparation time: 20 minutes
Cooking time: 30 minutes

Ingredients

Rice: 2½cups
Water: 1litre
Milk: 500ml
Butter: ½cup
Clove powder: 1tsp
Green cardamon powder: 1tsp
Boiled chickpea: 3½tbsp
Salt to taste

For Gatta

Besan: ¾cup
Yoghurt: ½cup
Water: 3½tbsp
Crushed peppercorn: ½tsp
Crushed whole coriander: ½tsp
Chilli powder: ½tsp
Turmeric powder: ½tsp
Salt to taste
Dough for sealing

Method

Mix besan, yoghurt, water, crushed peppercorns, crushed whole coriander, chilli powder, turmeric powder and salt into a dough.
Roll the dough into small dumplings.
Now boil the dumplings in water till they float.
Once boiled, let them cool.
Then fry them till golden brown.

For rice: Wash and soak rice in water for 10 minutes.
Prepare a mixture of water, milk, butter, clove powder and cardamon powder.
Now take a *lagan*, add rice and the mixture of milk and spices.
Put gatta dumplings in it and keep it on *dum* for 5–7 minutes.

DADHOJANAM

CHEF PRAVEEN ANAND, ITC HOTEL PARK SHERATON & TOWERS, CHENNAI

To serve: 2
Preparation time: 1 hour
Cooking time: 15 minutes

Ingredients

Rice: 2cups
Water: 2¼litres
Milk: 4cups
Yoghurt: 1½cup
Butter: 3½tbsp
Crushed pepper: 1tsp
Chopped ginger: 2tsp
Asafoetida powder: a pinch
Dry ginger: 1tsp
Ghee: 2tbsp
Red chilli: 1tsp
Mustard: ½tsp
Urad dal: 1tsp
Chana dal: 2tsp
Curry leaves: 1½tsp
Salt to taste

Method

Wash rice, strain and keep aside.
Bring water to a boil in a vessel, add rice. Cook till it is done.
Strain excess water and allow rice to cool.
Mix yoghurt, butter and salt.
Pour in cold milk, chopped ginger, asafoetida, crushed peppercorns and dry ginger powder.
Make a tempering of ghee with red chilli, mustard, dal and curry leaves.
Mix well and serve chilled.

KARIVEPILAI SAADAM

CHEF PRAVEEN ANAND, ITC HOTEL PARK SHERATON & TOWERS, CHENNAI

To serve: 2

Preparation time: 30 minutes

Cooking time: 15 minutes

Ingredients

Rice: 1½cup

Water: 2¼litres

To make the curry leaf powder

Curry leaves: 3½cups

Red chilli: 6

Urad dal: 2tsp

Asafoetida powder: a pinch

Salt to taste

For tempering

Gingelly oil (til ka tel): 4tbsp

Red chilli: 4

Mustard seeds: 1tsp

Urad dal: 2tsp

Chana dal: 1tsp

Curry leaves: a few sprigs

Method

Wash, strain and boil rice. Allow it to cool.

To make the curry leaf powder, broil or dry roast all ingredients, powder them and keep aside.

Heat oil in a separate *kadai* and temper with red chilli, mustard seeds, urad dal, chana dal and curry leaves in gingelly oil.

Add curry leaf powder and pour in the rice.

Check seasoning.

Serve hot.

CHINGRI MORICH PULAO

CHEF RAM, OH! CALCUTTA, DELHI

To serve: 6

Preparation time: 30 minutes

Cooking time: 40 minutes

Ingredients

Basmati rice: 2¼cups
Medium-sized prawns: 30pcs
Sliced onion: 4-5
Ginger paste: 3½tbsp
Black peppercorns: 4tsp
Freshly ground black pepper: 4tsp
Sliced green chilli: 2tsp
Bay leaves: 4-5
Diced tomato: ½cup
Lime juice: 1tbsp
Turmeric powder: 1tsp
Garam masala powder: 2/3tsp
Refined oil: 5tbsp
Ghee: 2tbsp
Salt to taste
Sugar to taste

Method

Pick and clean the rice under running water. Soak for 20 minutes.

Clean and devein the prawns, leaving the tails intact. Clean the prawn heads well.

Heat half of the refined oil in a pan, temper with 2 bay leaves and half of the peppercorns. Add some sliced onion and half of the ginger and sauté till the onion turns golden brown. Then add the cleaned prawn heads and sauté well.

Add 2 litres of water to the sautéed mixture and bring to a gentle boil. Then carefully skim the dirt that accumulates on the surface with a ladle. After that, cook till the stock is reduced to half.

Strain the stock and add the soaked rice and seasonings to it. Then bring to a boil and cook till the rice is three–fourth done. Drain the water and cool the cooked rice slightly.

In a wok, heat the rest of the oil and temper with peppercorns and bay leaves. When they begin to splutter, add the rest of the sliced onion and sauté. Then add the ginger paste and turmeric and sauté. When the oil leaves the sides of the wok, add the prawns, the rest of the spices and the diced tomatoes. Cook lightly and add to the cooked rice. From top, add the ghee, seasonings and lime juice. Mix everything lightly with a flat spoon.

GOAN FISH CRUSTED WITH RICE

CHEF ANDREW WHIFFEN, THE OBEROI, DELHI

To serve: 10

Preparation time: 30 minutes

Cooking time: 10 minutes

Ingredients

Fish fillet (mullet or snapper): 2kg
Ginger-garlic paste: 6tbsp
Red chilli paste: 5tbsp
Curry powder (mild): 2tsp
Goan toddy vinegar: 1½cup
Chopped fresh coriander: 2tbsp
Salt to taste
Roasted Basmati rice (crushed): 1½cup
Semolina: 2cups
Refined oil for shallow frying

Method

Clean the fish and dry it thoroughly.

Make a marination with ginger-garlic paste, red chilli paste, curry powder, toddy vinegar, coriander and salt.

Leave the fish to marinate in the above paste for 1–2 hours.

Mix the coarsely powdered rice and semolina and coat the marinated fish.

Shallow fry in oil till crisp and fish is cooked.

Serve hot with lemon wedges.

KOTHIMIRI MULAGU SAADAM

CHEF NABOJIT GHOSH, TAJ COROMANDEL, CHENNAI

To serve: 4

Preparation time: 7 minutes

Cooking time: 20 minutes

Ingredients

Basmati rice: 1½cup

Coriander leaves: 2bunches

Oil: ¼cup

Cumin seeds: 2tsp

Red chilli: 5

Curry leaves: a few

Urad dal: 1tsp

Black pepper: ½tsp

Salt to taste

Method

Grind the coriander leaves with oil, cumin seeds and dried red chillies to a paste.

Wash, soak and cook rice.

In a *handi*, heat oil and crackle mustard seeds, curry leaves, red chillies and urad dal.

Add the blended mixture to the *handi* and cook for some minutes.

Now add the cooked rice and stir well.

Garnish with curry leaves and serve hot.

ILISHER KHEYALI PULAO

CHEF RAM, OH! CALCUTTA, DELHI

To serve: 6

Preparation time: 1hour 30 minutes

Cooking time: 45 minutes

Ingredients

Hilsa fish: 1 whole

Basmati rice: 2¼cups

Sliced onion: 3 medium-sized onions

Ginger paste: 2½tbsp

Coriander powder: 1½tbsp

Green chilli paste: 3tbsp

Turmeric powder: 1tbsp

Mustard oil: ½cup

Slit green chilli: 6-8

Bay leaves: 2-3

Whole garam masala: 1tsp

Kewra water: 5-6drops

Salt to taste

Method

Clean the hilsa and cut into fillets carefully, reserving the bones and the head.

Smear the fillets with salt, turmeric, green chilli paste and mustard oil. Keep aside for 10 minutes.

Steam the marinated fish in the steamer. Remove from the steamer and cool. Reserve the oil from the fish.

Pick and soak the rice for 30 minutes.

Heat oil in a *kadai* and add the sliced onions. Sauté.

Add ginger, green chilli paste, turmeric powder and coriander powder. Cook over high heat. After a while, add the hilsa head and bones and sauté further. Then add the seasonings and kewra water. Pour in 2 litres of water and bring to a boil. Cook for 20 minutes to prepare a stock.

Strain the stock and discard the bones, reserve half of the stock and cook the other half till the stock is reduced to one-fourth. Remove from the fire and cool.

Add 1.5 litres of water to the reserved stock and bring to a boil. Drain the soaked rice and add to the boiling stock. Cook till three-fourth done.

Now debone the cooked hilsa fillet and make large dices.

In an earthen *handi*, put a layer of the cooked rice and a little of the reduced stock over the rice. Next put a layer of the deboned fish and slit green chillies. Cover with more rice and make similar layers.

After arranging the layers, seal the lid of the *handi* and bake in a preheated oven for 20 minutes. Serve hot.

BASMATI AND CORN KEBAB

CHEF ANDREW WHIFFEN, THE OBEROI, DELHI

To serve: 10
Preparation time: 45 minutes
Cooking time: 10-15 minutes

Ingredients

Natural unpolished Basmati rice: 1½cup
Corn: 5cups
Cardamom: 1tsp
Bay leaf: 1
Ginger julienne: 4tbsp
Chopped garlic: 2tbsp
Slit green chilli: 3
Coriander leaves: 3tbsp
Cumin seeds: 2tsp
Red chilli powder: 2tsp
Turmeric powder: 1tsp
Coriander powder: 2tsp
Cardamom powder: ½tsp
Mace powder: ½tsp
Ghee: ½cup
Salt to taste

Method

Heat ghee, add cumin seeds and stir until it crackles.
Add chopped garlic and stir till it turns a light brown colour.
Add ginger and green chillies and sauté for another 2 minutes.
Add red chillies, turmeric and coriander powder and stir for 30 seconds.
Take the corn, wash, soak overnight and boil in salted water with green cardamom, bay leaf, half of ginger, garlic and coriander root. Cool and mash the corn a little.
Add the corn and rice that has been washed, soaked for 4–5 hours and boiled in salted water.
Mix thoroughly and stir on a slow fire for 30 minutes. Adjust the seasoning.
Add cardamom and mace powder.
Remove from the fire and cool.
Shape the mixture into round cutlets of 2inch diameter and shallow fry in ghee until brown in colour and crisp. Serve hot with Mint Chutney, Laccha Onion and lemon wedges.

RICE AND ARTICHOKE FATAYAR

Chef Alok Anand, Taj Palace, Delhi

Makes: 30 pieces
Preparation time: 30 minutes
Cooking time: 15 minutes

Ingredients

Long grain rice: 1cup
Marinated artichokes: ¾cup
Grated Parmesan cheese: ¾cup
Olives: ¾cup
Fresh parsley: 1½tsp
Fresh basil: 2tsp
Chopped onion: 1
Chopped garlic: 2½tsp
Unsalted butter: ½cup
Phyllo sheets: 10

Method

Boil the rice in water and let it cool.
Preheat oven to 180°C.
Mix rice, chopped artichokes, Parmesan cheese, diced olives, sautéed onions and garlic, chopped herbs and melted butter.
Cut the phyllo sheets into 4inch circles.
Apply melted butter on one circle and place another circular sheet on top.
Place 1½tbsp of the rice mixture in the centre of the sheet, pinch the sheet from three sides and bring together to form a parcel.
Place on a greased baking sheet and bake in the preheated oven for 12–15 minutes or till golden brown.
Serve as an appetizer.

SMOKED BASMATI RICE TOPPED WITH MUSTARD BECKTI AND CRESS

CHEF SUJAN MUKHERJEE, TAJ BENGAL, KOLKATA

To serve: 4

Preparation time: 40 minutes

Cooking time: 30 minutes

Ingredients

Basmati rice: 1½cup
Chopped onion: 1 onion
Chopped garlic: ½tsp
Fresh red achari chilli: 2½tsp
Butter: 50gm
Fresh chives: 2½tsp
Pomegranate juice: ¼cup
Honey: 3tbsp
Raw Basmati rice for coating: ¼cup
Wood shredding: ½cup
Beckti fillet: 200gm
Pommery mustard: 2½tsp
Extra virgin olive oil: 1½tbsp
Gandharaj lemon: 1
Seasonings to adjust
Mustard cress: ½cup
Gandharaj lemon wedges: a few
Salt to taste
Black pepper powder to taste

Method

In a container, put the wood shredding, sprinkle honey and raw Basmati rice. Keep the container for boiling rice in the centre of the shavings. Light the shavings and cover the container with a tight-fitting lid.

In a separate pan, sauté the onion, garlic and fresh red chilli roundels with butter.

Add pomegranate juice. Allow to reduce.

Add the boiled Basmati and toss it nicely. Add fresh chopped chives. Adjust the seasoning.

Heat oil, sear the fillet, sprinkle the seasonings and put in the oven till it is cooked.

Rub mustard and lemon juice on the fillet and place on the rice.

Place the smoked rice on the centre of the plate and keep the fish on top of the rice.

Reduce the pomegranate juice and slowly pour the extra virgin olive oil in it.

Serve and garnish with pomegranate oil and mustard cress.

JOHN DORY WITH RICE GATEAUX AND RED WINE FIVE SPICE REDUCTION

CHEF ANDREW WHIFFEN, THE OBEROI, DELHI

To serve: 10

Preparation time: 30 minutes

Cooking time: 45 minutes

Ingredients

Basmati rice: 3cups
Wild rice: ½cup
Peeled garlic: 8-10 cloves
Extra virgin olive oil: ½cup
Fish stock: 1½cup
Chicken stock: ½cup
Red wine: 4½tbsp
Five-spice powder: 1tsp
John Dory fillet: 1½ kg
Salt to taste
Butter: 400gm

Method

Soak the Basmati rice and wild rice. Boil them separately and mix them together.

Sauté garlic in olive oil and add the rice mixture to it. Cook till the moisture evaporates. Remove from the flame.

Shape the rice mixture into rounds of 2inch diameter.

Reduce the fish stock and chicken stock with the red wine. Add five-spice powder and strain through a fine cloth.

Clean the fish and dry it thoroughly.

Add salt to the fish and fry the fish in butter till the skin becomes crisp.

Shallow fry in oil till the fish is cooked and turns crisp.

Stack the fish on top of the rice cakes and drizzle the sauce over it.

BASMATI RICE COATED MEAT DUMPLINGS

CHEF NABOJIT GHOSH, TAJ COROMANDEL, CHENNAI

To serve: 4

Preparation time: 15 minutes

Cooking time: 25 minutes

Ingredients

Basmati rice: ½cup

Minced lamb: 1½cup

Green chilli: 3

Eggs: 2

Cornflour: 5tbsp

Celery: ¼cup

Maida to dust

Salt to taste

Method

Double mince the lamb.

Prepare a separate mixture of egg, cornflour and chopped celery.

Bind the mixture with minced lamb and salt.

Coat the meat balls with Basmati rice and sprinkle flour over them.

Cook the dumplings in a steamer and serve with Hot Garlic Sauce.

MUSHROOM BASMATI RICE CAKES

CHEF ANUP GUPTA, TAJ LANDS END, MUMBAI

To serve: 4

Preparation time: 30 minutes

Cooking time: 35-40 minutes

Ingredients

Brown rice: 2cups
Basmati rice: 1cup
Manicured shallots: ½cup
Sliced spring onion: ½cup
Sliced Shiitake mushroom: 1½cup
Shiitake stock: 8cups
Sliced morel mushroom: ¼cup
Sliced shallots: ½cup
Olive oil: ¼cup
Mirin: 1tbsp
Green peas: 5cups
Snow peas: 3cups
Chopped ginger: ½cup
Black sesame seeds: 2tbsp
White sesame seeds: 2tbsp
Thinly sliced spring onions (kept in ice bath): 1cup
Salt to taste
Pepper to taste

Method

Boil the rice in mushroom stock and add salt to it.

Slice shiitake, morel and shallots.

Juice the green peas and snow peas separately. Mix equal quantity of them and heat in the double boiler.

Heat it until both the juices reach a thin, sauce-like consistency. While preparing the pea sauce, keep the heat low to prevent it from disintegrating.

Slice ginger and mix it with mirin. Heat the mirin mixture and mix with the peas sauce.

Reduce the mushroom stock and make a ragout of morels and shiitake by sautéing shallots and then the mushrooms. Mix in the reduced stock.

Mix the green onions and manicured shallots with the equal quantity of rice and add seasonings to it. Take the cake of the rice mixture and coat it with black and white sesame seeds.

In a pan, sear the rice cakes until it turns golden brown and smells nutty.

In a deep plate, place the cakes along each other. Pour the sauce all around the cake, dipping it one-fourth from bottom.

Top the cakes with the sautéed mushrooms and garnish with the thinly sliced spring onions.

Serve mildly hot.

SAFFRON CORIANDER BASMATI RICE WITH FRESH ASPARAGUS CAGE AND BASIL OIL

CHEF SUJAN MUKHERJEE, TAJ BENGAL, KOLKATA

To serve: 4
Preparation time: 20 minutes
Cooking time: 30 minutes

Ingredients

Basmati rice: 1½cup
Saffron: a pinch
Chopped onion: 4
Chopped garlic: 1tsp
Butter: 50gm
Double cream: ¼cup
Coriander leaves: a bunch
Seasonings to adjust
Salt to taste

For the cage

Asparagus tips: 1cup
Iceberg lettuce: ½cup
Scallion (tar knot): 2
Fresh basil: ½cup
Extra virgin olive oil: ¼cup
Cherry tomato: ¼cup
Scallion tips: 8
Coriander leaves: 4 sprigs

Method

Roast the saffron strands and dilute with water to make a nice paste.

Sauté onions and garlic in butter. To it, add the saffron paste, rice and seasonings and finish with coriander leaves and cream.

To make the cage, blanch the asparagus and cut it lengthwise from top to bottom. Then sauté it in extra virgin olive oil and add seasonings.

To make the oil, fry the basil leaves in extra virgin olive oil, purée it and strain.

Place the rice on the centre of the plate and place the cage (filled with iceberg lettuce) on top of the rice.

Garnish and serve with stewed cherry tomatoes, scallion tips, coriander leaves and basil oil. Serve warm.

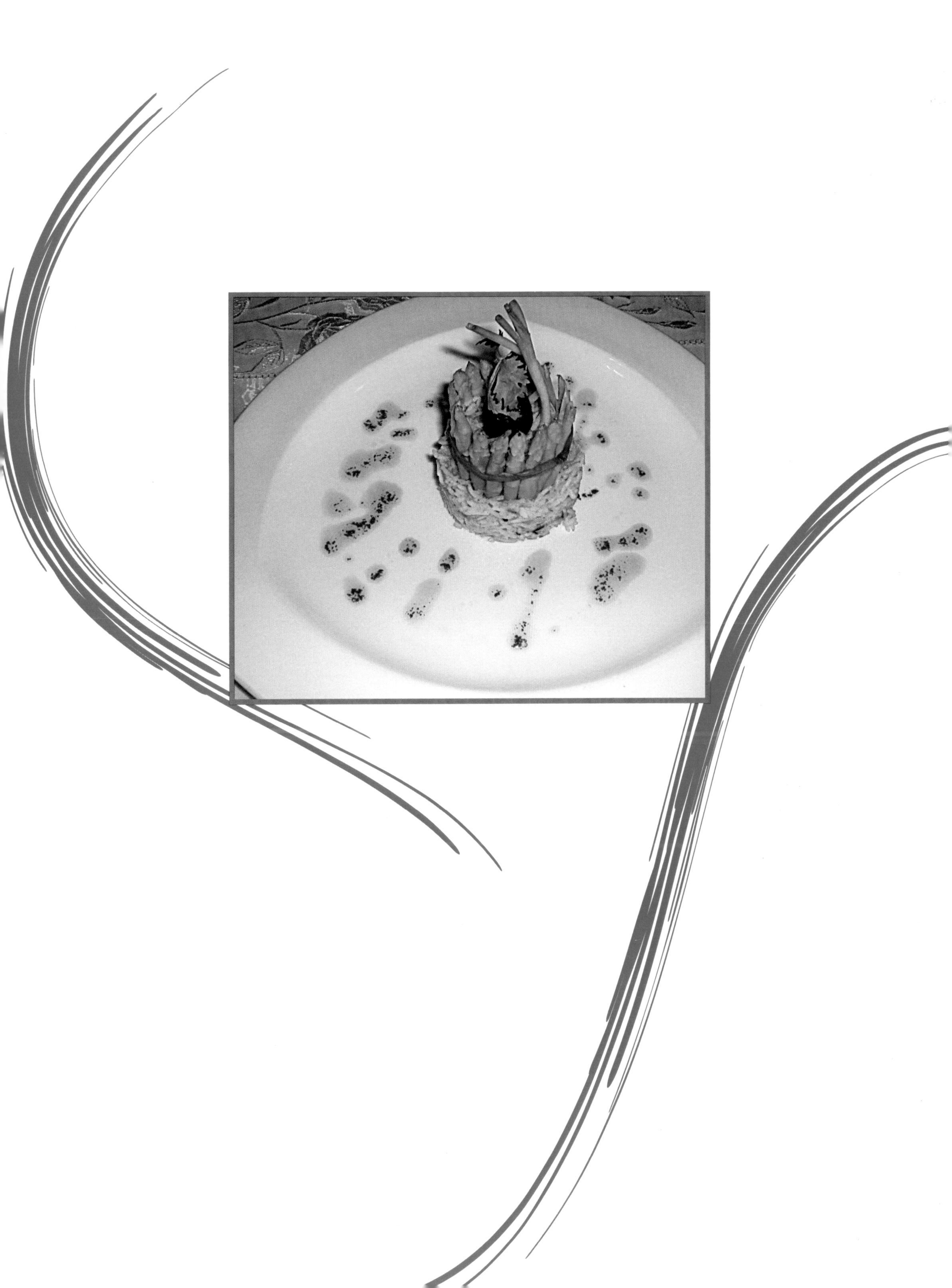

KEDGEREE

Chef Andrew Whiffen, The Oberoi, Delhi

To serve: 5
Preparation time: 20 minutes
Cooking time: 25-30 minutes

Ingredients

Smoked haddock fillet: 450gm
Butter: 100gm
Refined oil: 2tbsp
Chopped onion: 3-4 medium-sized onions
Basmati rice: 1½cup
Curry powder (mild): 2tsp
Peas: ¾cup
Poached eggs: 5
Chopped parsley: 1tbsp
Salt to taste
Black pepper powder to taste

Method

Cover the haddock with boiling water and leave for 5 minutes. Drain, reserving the soaking liquid.
Measure the soaking liquid and add water to make it up to 600ml.
Skin and flake the haddock, removing bones you come across. Set aside.
Melt half the butter with the oil in a large saucepan. Add the onion and cook gently until softened but not browned.
Add the rice and curry powder and stir for 1-2 minutes.
Pour in the measured cooking liquid, bring it to a boil, then reduce heat down to a bare simmer and cover tightly.
Leave to cook, without disturbing for 8 minutes and then stir in the flaked haddock and the peas.
Cover and simmer for a further 4-5 minutes, until the rice is tender and has absorbed all the liquid.
Remove the pan from the heat, dot the rice with the remaining butter and let it stand for 4 minutes.
Add parsley and stir in lightly with a fork, fluffing up the grains of rice.
Taste and adjust seasoning, adding salt only if needed.
Serve garnished with poached eggs.

BASMATI CRUSTED CRAB CAKES

CHEF ANDREW WHIFFEN, THE OBEROI, DELHI

To serve: 10

Preparation time: 45 minutes

Cooking time: 10-15 minutes

Ingredients

Basmati rice: 1½cup
Crabmeat: 9cups
Chopped onion: 5 medium-sized onions
Kasundi (mustard paste): ¾cup
Ginger julienne: 4tbsp
Slit green chilli: 2tbsp
Chopped coriander leaves: 3tbsp
Red chilli powder: 2tsp
Turmeric powder: 1tsp
Cumin powder: 3tsp
Eggs: 5
Oil to deep fry
Salt to taste

Method

Mash the crabmeat and mix it with kasundi and chopped vegetables.
Mould into small, round cakes.
Dip the cakes in egg batter and coat with roasted and crushed rice.
Deep fry till the crab cakes turn brown.
Serve with Mint Chutney and Onion Laccha.

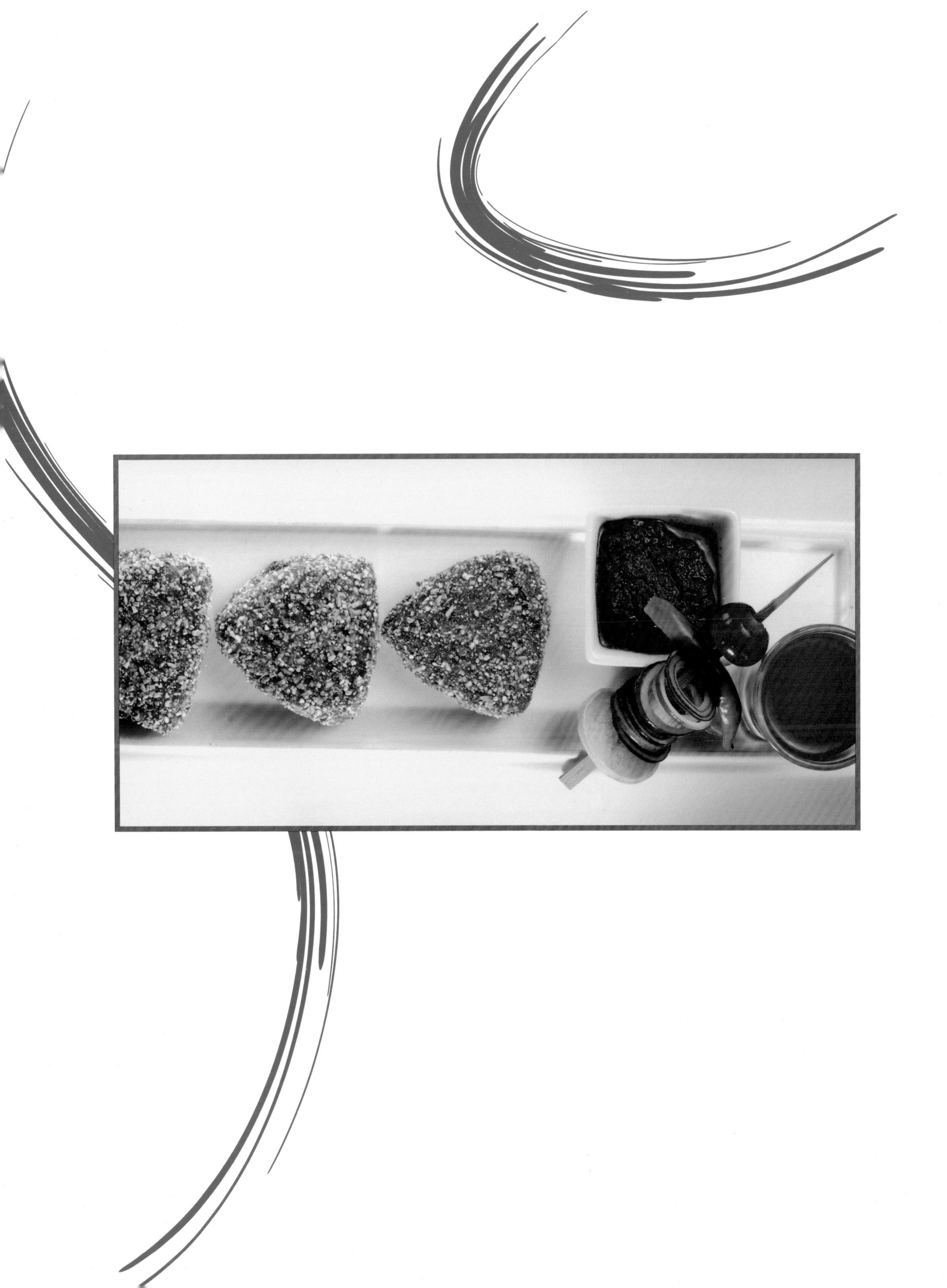

SHRIMP AND CHICKEN JAMBALAYA

Chef Ramesh Javvaji, ITC Sonar, Kolkata

To serve: 4
Preparation time: 2 hours
Cooking time: 45 minutes

Ingredients

Unsalted butter: 10tbsp
Onion: 5
Bell pepper: 5
Celery: 2tbsp
Fresh tomatoes: 8 medium-sized tomatoes
Tomato sauce: 1½tbsp
Long grain Basmati rice: 2cups
Chicken stock: 5cups
Worcestershire sauce: 4tbsp
Minced garlic: 1½tbsp
Diced chicken: 1tbsp
Shrimp: 1tbsp
Parsley: ½cup
Sliced green onions: 2tbsp

To make the seasoning mix

White pepper: 1tsp
Salt: ½tsp
Thyme: ½tsp
Rubbad sage: 2tsp
Dried basil: 3tsp
Black pepper: 1tsp

Method

Mix onion, celery and bell pepper (the Holy Trinity) together.

In a cast iron Dutch oven, melt the butter over medium heat, add half of the Holy Trinity and cook until the vegetables are tender.

Add diced tomatoes and cook for 1 minute.

Add tomato sauce and cook for another minute.

Add Basmati rice and cook for 2 minutes, stirring constantly. Put the stock, the remaining of the Holy Trinity, the seasoning mix, Worcestershire, and garlic.

Taste the broth for seasoning, particularly salt.

Add chicken, stir well and put the pot in the preheated oven. Bake uncovered for 25 minutes.

Then stir in the raw shrimp, parsley, and green onions and place back in the oven for an additional 10 minutes or until the shrimps are cooked thoroughly.

SALMON MISO WITH TEPPAYAKI FRIED RICE

CHEF ANDREW WHIFFEN, THE OBEROI, DELHI

To serve: 4

Preparation time: 1 hour

Cooking time: 25-30 minutes

Ingredients

Salmon: 150gm
Cooked Japanese rice: 2tbsp
Brown Basmati rice: 2tbsp
Chopped red capsicum: 1tsp
Chopped yellow capsicum: 1tsp
Chopped green capsicum: 1tsp
Chopped carrot: 1tsp
Chopped onion: 1tsp
Soya (Kikkoman): 1tsp
Wakame (a type of seaweed): 1tsp
Takuan (Japanese pickle): 1tsp
Cucumber julienne: 1tsp

For the Saikyo Miso:
Mirin (Japanese rice wine): 2tbsp
Sake (Japanese beverage): 2tbsp
White Miso paste: 4-5tbsp
Sugar: 5tbsp

Method

Bring the sake and mirin to a boil in a saucepan over high heat for 20 seconds. Evaporate the alcohol. Turn the heat down to low.

Add the miso paste, using a wooden spatula. Dissolve it completely, turn the heat up to high and add sugar. Stir constantly to ensure that the bottom of the pan does not burn. Remove from the heat once the sugar has dissolved. Cool to room temperature.

Now preheat the oven to 200°C.

Preheat the grill and lightly wipe off any excess miso clinging to the fillet. Place the fish on the grill. Grill until the surface of the fish turns brown. Bake for 10–12 minutes.

Cook the combined brown and Japanese rice in a flat grill, mixing the vegetables together. Cook for 5 minutes.

Arrange the fish and the rice together and garnish with pickled radish and cucumber juliennes.

Add extra drops of miso sauce to the plate.

NASI GORENG

CHEF ANDREW WHIFFEN, THE OBEROI, DELHI

To serve: 10
Preparation time: 45 minutes
Cooking time: 8-10 minutes

Ingredients

Basmati rice: 3½cups
Peeled garlic: 1cup
Chopped onions: 1cup
Peeled prawns: 3cups
Dried shrimp paste: 3tbsp
Aromat (seasoning powder): 3tbsp
Thai dark soya sauce: 4tbsp
Sugar: 3tbsp
Fresh basil: 1cup
Spring onions: 1cup
Refined oil: 1cup

Method

Soak the rice for 30 minutes and boil it till it is almost cooked.

Cool and stir the rice with a fork to separate the grains.

Heat oil in the wok and fry the onions, garlic, prawns and shrimp paste until the prawns are cooked.

Now add the rice, seasoning, sugar and soya sauce. Add a little oil if necessary. Stir constantly until well mixed and heated through.

Garnish with fried egg and serve with Chicken Satay and Shrimp Crackers.

GRILLED SCALLOPS WITH ONIGIRI

CHEF ANDREW WHIFFEN, THE OBEROI, DELHI

To serve: 10

Preparation time: 45 minutes

Cooking time: 1 hour

Ingredients

Scallops: 160gm
Japanese rice: 3tbsp
Brown Basmati rice: 3tbsp
Salmon egg: 1tsp
Saikyo miso: 4tbsp
Mitsukan vinegar: 1tbsp
Wasabi powder: 1tsp
Water: 1tsp
Wakame (a type of seaweed): 1tsp
Leek juliennes for garnishing

Method

Cook scallops for 2-3 minutes over high heat with a little oil. Use a non-stick frying pan.

Dissolve the wasabi powder in a bowl containing hot water. Add the saikyo miso and Mitsukan vinegar and mix well. Then add some chopped wakame to make the sauce.

In a plate, pour the sauce. Top it with the fried scallops and fried leeks.

For the onigiri, combine Basmati brown rice and Japanese rice, both of which have been soaked overnight.

Cook the rice combination for 30 minutes in a pressure cooker. Let it cool for 15 minutes.

Take a handful of cooked rice, put the salmon eggs inside and mould into a triangular shape.

Then place it on the centre of the plate together with the scallops. Serve.

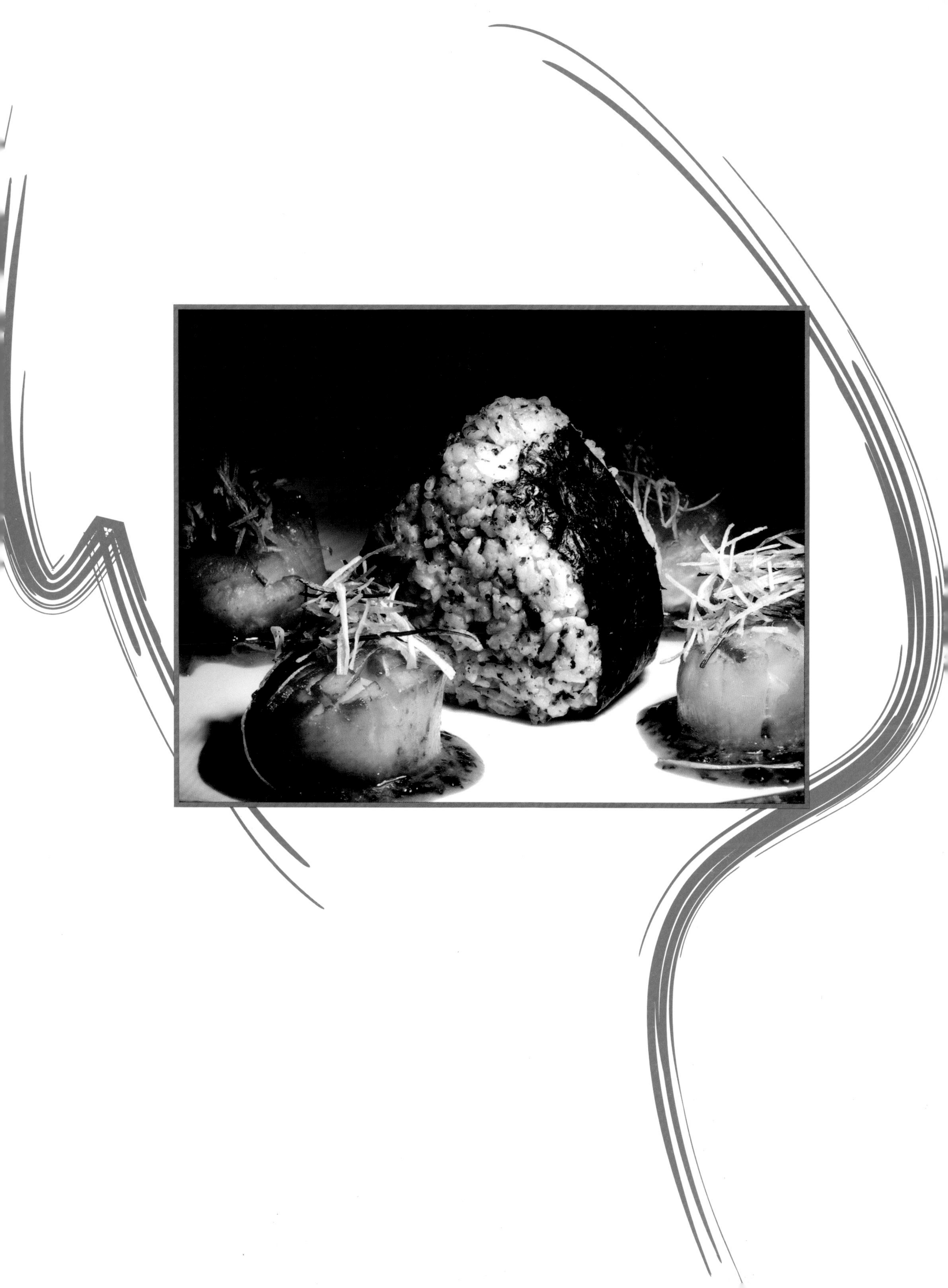

KHAO PAD KAPROW KAI

Chef Nitin Pal Singh, Oriental Octopus, India Habitat Centre, Delhi

To serve: 2

Preparation time: 40 minutes

Cooking time: 10 minutes

Ingredients

Boiled Basmati rice: 1½cup
Refined Oil: 2tbsp
Garlic: 4tsp
Fresh red chilli: 2 small chillies
Kafir lime leaves: 1-2 leaves
Minced chicken: ½cup
Fish sauce: 2tsp
Oyster sauce: 1tbsp
Dark soya sauce: 1tsp
Sugar: 1tsp
White pepper powder: a pinch
Basil leaves: 8–12 leaves
Vegetable stock: 4tsp

Method

Heat oil in a *kadai*. Saute chopped garlic, kafir lime leaves and chopped fresh red chilli.
Add stock, oyster sauce, fish sauce, sugar and white pepper powder. Mix well.
Add minced chicken and stir-fry till done.
Again add boiled rice, dark soya sauce and basil leaves. Stir-fry over high heat.
Serve hot.

THAI BASIL FRIED RICE WITH CHICKEN

Chef Nitin Pal Singh, Oriental Octopus, India Habitat Centre, Delhi

To serve: 2

Preparation time: 30 minutes

Cooking time: 10 minutes

Ingredients

Boiled Basmati rice: 1½cup
Refined oil: 1tbsp
Chopped garlic: 1tbsp
Thai chilli paste: 4tsp
Fish sauce: 1tbsp
Oyster sauce: 2tsp
Sugar: 1tsp
Chicken breast: ¼cup
Basil leaves: 8–12 leaves
White pepper powder: a pinch
Soya sauce: 1tsp
Vegetable stock: 4tsp

Method

Cut chicken into juliennes and using a little amount of oil, stir-fry them till done.

Heat oil in a *kadai* and sauté garlic and Thai chilli paste together over medium heat.

Add fish sauce, oyster sauce, sugar and mix well.

Add the stock, chicken juliennes, boiled rice, white pepper powder, dark soya sauce and toss well.

Add basil leaves and stir-fry over high heat. Serve hot.

PRAWN FRIED RICE WITH LEMONGRASS

CHEF NITIN PAL SINGH, ORIENTAL OCTOPUS, INDIA HABITAT CENTRE, DELHI

To serve: 2

Preparation time: 30 minutes

Cooking time: 10 minutes

Ingredients

Boiled rice: 1½cup
Refined oil: 2tbsp
Galangal: 1 small piece
Lemongrass: ½ a stick
Garlic: 1tbsp
Egg: 1
Prawn: ½cup
Oyster sauce: 2tsp
Fish sauce: 1tbsp
Sugar: 1tsp
White pepper powder: a pinch
Spring onion: 1½tbsp
Sambal chilli paste: 2tsp
Vegetable stock: 4tsp

Method

Peel and devein prawns and cut lengthwise.

Heat oil in a wok and stir-fry prawns till done. Keep aside.

Again heat oil in a wok and sauté chopped garlic, chopped galangal and finely chopped lemongrass over a medium heat. Add beaten egg and scramble it.

Add fish sauce, oyster sauce, sugar, white pepper powder and chilli paste sambal. Mix well.

Add stock, prawns, boiled rice and spring onion.

Stir-fry over high heat and serve hot.

RICE LADDOO

CHEF RAJESH WADHWA, TAJ PALACE HOTEL, DELHI

Makes: 35 pieces

Preparation time: 25 minutes

Cooking time: 5 minutes

Ingredients

Steamed long-grained rice: 1¼cup
Ghee: 3tbsp
Sugar: ¾cup
Saffron strands: about 30
Pistachio slivers: 3½tsp
Silver foil for garnishing
Cherry for garnishing

Method

Lightly sauté the steamed rice, add the sugar syrup and cook.

Divide the mixture into small portions and roll in the shape of round balls.

Garnish with silver foil, pistachio slivers, saffron strands and cherries.

ARI PAYASAM

Chef Nabojit Ghosh, Taj Coromandel, Chennai

To serve: 4

Preparation time: 40 minutes

Cooking time: 10 minutes

Ingredients

Basmati rice: 1cup
Milk: 2litres
Condensed milk: 1½cup
Ghee: 3tbsp
Cashew nut: 2tbsp
Raisin: 2tbsp
Pistachio to garnish
Sugar to taste

Method

Parboil the rice and strain.

Boil the milk and condense it. Add condensed milk and sugar, and stir.

Then add the parboiled rice and cook till it is done.

Heat ghee in a pan and fry the cashew nuts and raisins.

Pour the nuts into the payasam.

Garnish with pistachios and serve hot.

CHILGOZA KHEER

CHEF I S RAWAT, JAYPEE RESIDENCY MANOR, MUSSOORIE

To serve: 4

Preparation time: 30 minutes

Cooking time: 25 minutes

Ingredients

Basmati rice: ¾cup

Jaggery: 2½cups

Pinenuts or chilgoza: ¾cup

Full cream milk: 2litres

Water: 500ml

Method

Take milk in a heavy-bottomed pan. Add soaked rice and bring to a boil. Simmer over a low flame till the rice is almost cooked.

Dissolve jaggery in water, boil it for 10 minutes, strain, and keep aside.

Add strained jaggery water and chilgoza. Stir the milk continuously for 5–10 minutes and let it reduce further.

Remove the pan from the fire and pour the kheer in a bowl.

Garnish the kheer with the remaining chilgoza. Serve hot.

ZAFFRANI KHEER

CHEF YOGESH ARORA, TIFFIN ROOM, RAFFLES HOTEL, SINGAPORE

To serve: 5-6

Preparation time: 45 minutes

Cooking time: 25-30 minutes

Ingredients

Fresh milk: 1½litres
Basmati rice: ½cup
Brown unrefined sugar: 1cup
Green cardamom powder: ½tsp
Roasted and sliced almond: 2tsp
Sliced pistachio: 2tsp
Dry apricot: 1½tsp
Roasted and sliced almond and cashew nut: 1½tbsp
Raisin: 1tbsp
Saffron: a pinch

Method

In a heavy-bottomed, stainless-steel pot, bring the milk to a boil and add saffron to the boiling milk.
Add rice that has been washed and soaked. Mix well.
Stir constantly so that the rice does not stick to the bottom of the pot.
Check to see if the rice is cooked through.
Once the rice is almost cooked, add sugar, cardamom powder and the dry fruits. Serve warm or chilled.

MANJARI CHOCOLATE PHIRNI WITH PISTACHIO CRUNCH

CHEF ANDREW WHIFFEN, THE OBEROI, DELHI

To serve: 10

Preparation time: 20 minutes

Cooking time: 1 hour

Ingredients

Milk: 2litres

Sugar: 1½cup

Basmati rice: 1cup

Valrohna chocolate (Manjari): 1½cup

Pistachio: 3tbsp

Method

Soak the rice and make it into a paste.

Boil the milk. Add sugar to the boiled milk.

Add the rice paste to the milk and keep stirring till a thick mass is formed.

Remove from the flame. Then add chocolate and pistachio.

Pour the mixture in desired moulds and chill thoroughly.

Serve chilled, garnished with pistachios.

ZARDA PULAO

CHEF AMIT CHOWDHURY, THE TAJ MAHAL HOTEL, DELHI

To serve: 4

Preparation time: 20 minutes

Cooking time: 25 minutes

Ingredients

Basmati rice: 1½cup
Saffron: a small pinch
Ghee: ½cup
Cashew nuts: 20
Raisin: 2tbsp
Sugar: about ½cup
Khoya: ¼cup
Rose water: ½tbsp
Milk: about ½cup
Dough for sealing

Method

Soak the rice in water for 1-2 hours.

In ghee, fry cashew nuts and raisins to a golden brown.

Drain the water from the rice. Heat 500ml of water in a *handi*. Add saffron and milk and bring to a boil. Then add the rice and let it boil further.

Reduce the heat and let the rice cook till it is three-fourth done. The rice will take the saffron colour.

Take another deep pan or *handi*. Put one-fourth the quantity of boiled rice in it. Sprinkle some sugar, khoya and fried nuts on top of the boiled rice. Put 20ml of ghee. Now make the second layer by adding half of the remaining rice. Layer it with sugar, nuts and ghee.

Finally, pour in the remaining ghee and rose water and put a silver foil on top.

Seal the *handi* to put it on *dum*.

Preheat the oven to 175°C.

Keep the *handi* on *dum* in the oven for 12–15 minutes.

Leave aside for some time.

Open the lid, serve on a platter, garnished with silver foil and nuts.

YAKHNI JOLER PULAO

Chef Ram, Oh! Calcutta, Delhi

To serve: 6

Preparation time: 1hour 30 minutes

Cooking time: 25 minutes

Ingredients

Basmati rice: 2½cups
Ghee: ⅔cup
Cashew nut: 4½tbsp
Raisin: 3½tbsp
Bay leaves: 4-5
Black peppercorn: 1½tbsp
White peppercorn: 1tbsp
Green cardamom: 1½tbsp
Black cardamom: 1½tbsp
Mace: 1tsp
Nutmeg: ½ of a whole
Cloves: 2tsp
Cinnamon: 1½tbsp
Fennel seeds: 1tbsp
Coriander seeds: 2tbsp
Cumin seeds: 2tsp
Whole turmeric: 1½tbsp
Whole red chilli: 2
Saffron: ½tsp
Milk: ½cup
Rose water: 1tsp
Salt to taste
Sugar to taste
Rose petals for garnishing
Dough for sealing

Method

In a large pan, put all the whole spices and add about 3 litres of water. Bring to a gentle boil and simmer for 1 hour. The quantity of the liquid should be twice the quantity of rice. Strain and simmer.

Pick and soak the rice for 20 minutes. Then drain and dry the rice for 10 minutes.

Heat ghee in a heavy-bottomed pan. Add bay leaves and cashew nut and sauté lightly. Then add the rice and sauté till the rice is coated with ghee.

Pour the simmering spice stock over the sautéed rice and mix well. Add salt and raisins. Bring to a boil.

After that, dissolve the saffron in milk and add to the rice. Then add a little rose water. Mix well and cook on high heat till the water dries up and the rice is almost done. Add a little sugar and mix in.

Put the pan on *dum* and place a heavy weight on the lid to prevent steam and the flavours from escaping.

Cook the rice on *dum* for 10 minutes. Then mix the rice with a flat spoon. Serve hot.

CHAMELI KHUSKA

CHEF PRAVEEN ANAND, ITC HOTEL PARK SHERATON & TOWERS, CHENNAI

To serve: 2

Preparation time: 45 minutes

Cooking time: 15 minutes

Ingredients

Fresh jasmine flower: 2cups

Basmati rice: 1½cup

Water: 3¾cups

Method

Wash rice, strain and keep aside.

Remove the stems and tie the jasmine flowers in a muslin cloth.

Bring water to a boil. Infuse the essence of the flowers by dipping the muslin in the boiling water.

Then put in the washed rice and cook till done.

Serve hot.